THE ROBIE HOUSE

THE ROBIE HOUSE
OF FRANK LLOYD WRIGHT

THE UNIVERSITY OF CHICAGO PRESS · CHICAGO AND LONDON

□ □ □ □ □ JOSEPH CONNORS □ □ □ □ □

Works in Chicago Architecture and Urbanism are published
in honor of Ann Lorenz Van Zanten and are supported in
part by a fund established in her memory at the Chicago
Historical Society, where she was curator of Architectural
Collections until her death in 1982.

Joseph Connors is associate professor of
art history at Columbia University.

Photograph of Robie House on title page
reproduced courtesy of H. B. Barnard Co.

The University of Chicago Press, Chicago 60637
The University of Chicago Press, Ltd., London

Library of Congress Cataloging in Publication Data

Connors, Joseph.
    The Robie House of Frank Lloyd Wright.

    Bibliography: p.
    Includes index.
    1. Robie House (Chicago, Ill.) 2. Organic archi-
tecture—Illinois—Chicago. 3. Chicago (Ill.)—
Dwellings. 4. Wright, Frank Lloyd, 1867–1959.
I. Title.
NA7238.C4C65   1983   728.8'3'0924   83-4891
ISBN 0-226-11541-0 (cloth)
ISBN 0-226-11542-9 (pbk.)

To Joe, Marilyn, and Martha Locker
and in memory of Catherine

CONTENTS

□ □ □ □ PREFACE □ □ □ □

This book is written for the layman who would like to take a close look at a single house by Frank Lloyd Wright. It describes the Robie House as it stands today at 58th Street and Woodlawn Avenue in Hyde Park. But it also tries to do something riskier, to recapture what went on in the creative moment when the house was designed sometime between 1906 and 1909. The house now looks so familiar and inevitable that it takes an effort of the imagination to recall that the design was once fluid and tentative, and that many possibilities lay open to the architect. To evoke this stage I have relied extensively on Wright's own writings as well as on a few of the rare working drawings that survive from this period of his career. For the layman whose eye is sharpened by this exercise and who wants to know more, I have included a basic bibliography. The Wright specialist and other architectural historians will soon be able to turn to the definitive monograph on the Robie House now being prepared by Donald Hoffmann.

Mr. William Barnard, son of the original contractor of the house, has earned the gratitude of all students of Wright by his generous donation of construction photographs and other materials to the University of Chicago. I owe the modern photographs reproduced here to the kindness and skill of Margaret Olin. I am grateful to Professor John Van Vleck for an inspiring evening discussing Wright when I was first starting out, and to Professor Neil Harris for sharing his extensive knowledge of Wright's America. Katherine Lee Keefe and Mary Bartholomew kindly provided information and photographs. Dr. John Moran and Mrs. Maya Moran showed what it is like to live in a Wright house with sensitivity and imagination. The manuscript benefited from a long conversation with David and Ann Van Zanten; her help can only be remembered now with sadness. I am very grateful to my father, Thomas Connors, for clarifying many points of structure and design on an enlightening walk through the house.

I began this book when I was a member of the University of Chicago community, and finished it with fond memories of the many friends who live in walking distance from the Robie House. I hope they will enjoy it.

Figure 1. Robie House, side along 58th Street, looking north (Richard Nickel)

INTRODUCTION

The Robie House confounds expectations of what a house should look like (figs. 1–3). It has no street facade and no obvious door. There are hardly any solid walls. Instead, it seems to be a building assembled out of giant blocks, free-floating roofs, and endless ribbons of windows. The distinguishing feature by which the house is immediately recognized is the famous cantilevered roof that extends twenty feet beyond the last masonry support and provokes the troubling thought that no wooden roof could possibly extend that far for long. Its relentlessly straight lines make the house look like the least natural of objects. It shuns the foliate ornament and historical detail that characterize the other houses on the block, most of which were constructed from progressive designs of the decade immediately preceding that of the Robie House, 1900 to 1909. Its only ornament seems to be the abstract patterns in its windows and hundreds of flowers that blossom in season from planters hidden in nearly every horizontal ledge. Peering through the screen of plants and glass, one wonders where the inhabitants could possibly live. Comparing the house with its generous and graceful neighbors, one senses a sharp social break, a tone of emphatic dissent. On a street of large, stately houses the Robie House looks small and severe

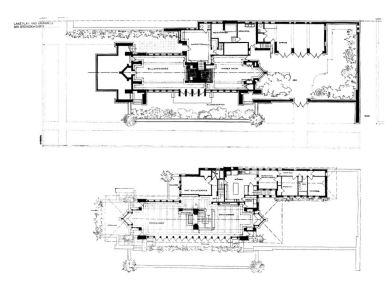

Figure 2. Robie House, plans of ground floor and main floor (Wasmuth 1911)

and, one might rashly judge, cheap, like an interloper from a different class, a mechanic among the gentry.

A few houses of the previous generation had experimented with similar ideas, but comparisons serve merely to show how distinctive the Robie House really is, and how complete was its rupture with convention. One house that looks at first glance like a precursor is the Lyman Joseph House in Newport, Rhode Island, built by the architect Clarence Luce in 1882–83 (fig. 4).[1] With hindsight the Joseph House seems to be edging in the Robie direction. The roof has a prismatic quality and an air of independence from the spaces beneath it. It is not cantilevered, but the posts that support it in front are so thin that it is easy to miss them and see, instead, a long, horizontal roof hovering over a bay window of glass. This image is restated more succinctly in the tiny well that stands in front of the porch and seems like an abstraction of the larger house, for it has a stony base and a prismatic roof with minimal support. In comparison with the Robie House, however, the Joseph House still looks casual, humane, and old-fashioned. The Robie House is so obviously an extreme statement that it makes us pose two questions: what could have been going through the mind of Frank Lloyd Wright when he designed it, and who was this man Robie who commissioned it?

Figure 3. Robie House (Margaret Olin)
Figure 4. Lyman Joseph House, Newport, Rhode Island, by Clarence Luce, 1882–83 (Sheldon, *Artistic Country-Seats,* 1886)

Figure 5. Robie House in construction, with the Robies in front, 1909 (H. B. Barnard Co.)

In 1906 Frederick C. Robie was a thirty-year-old engineer, about ten years younger than his architect. He was born in 1876 and educated at the Yale School in Chicago and the Chicago Manual Training School, and in 1896 he took an engineering degree at Purdue. Between 1901 and 1909 he worked for his father's firm, the Excelsior Supply Company, which at first made bicycles but gradually diversified into auto- mobile supplies. In 1905 Frederick rose to the position of assistant manager, while in 1908 he formed another automobile supply company with his father, the Factory Sales Corporation. He became president of Excelsior in 1910, after his father's death, but the business failed in 1912 and was bought out by Schwinn. Robie's marriage failed as well, and after only two years of Robie occupancy, the house was sold, and Frederick Robie disappeared from the scene until 1958, when he was found by the *Architectural Forum* and interviewed about the famous house to which his name had become inextricably attached.[2]

If bicycles were Robie's first business, his passion was the automobile, and perhaps the most significant fact we know about him was that he produced a prototype for an early engine-driven runabout.[3] Thus Robie fits into the large class

Figure 6. Frank Lloyd Wright
(Metropolitan Museum of Art, Edward
Pearce Casey Fund, 1982.

of bicycle manufacturers who turned to the production of cars in the early years of the century, and one does in fact find his name in the list of the 2,200 automobile makers who functioned in America prior to 1925.[4] He was one of the hundreds of new entrants into the industry who never became established. But his interest in cars explains certain features of the house, like the three-car garage with a built-in car wash and a pit for working on engines.[5] More importantly, the automobile was a link with Wright. The architect loved cars and had a Stoddard Dayton sportscar custom built to his own design (which included a cantilevered convertible roof).[6] Furthermore, it is interesting to note that the years of Wright's classic achievement, the Prairie House, coincide with the birth of the American automobile. The first American gasoline car was built in 1893, the year of Wright's first major independent commission, the Winslow House. Ford's first car was built in 1896, and the Ford Motor Company was founded in 1903. The early Oldsmobiles were produced in 1901–4, Ford's low-priced Model N in 1906, the Model T in 1908, and the Ford assembly line for mass production was moving by 1909. The years 1903–11, which bracket the Robie House, saw intense litigation between the holders of the Selden patent on the internal combustion automobile and challengers like Ford. And in 1908–9 there was a rush of newcomers into the industry. Hundreds of companies sprang up, and hundreds disappeared.[7] What Robie shared with these many small entrepreneurs, and also with Wright, was the mentality of the inventor. As Robie put it: "I contacted him, and from the first we had a definite community of thought. When I talked in mechanical terms, he talked and thought in architectural terms. I thought, well, he was in my world."[8]

The interest in mechanics was a trait Robie shared with many of Wright's clients. Wright himself characterized these men as "businessmen with unspoiled instincts and untainted ideals," and more recently Leonard Eaton has drawn a convincing profile of the typical Wright client in the period up to 1910.[9] Many were managers in small and medium sized companies, and often they were concerned with the mechanical side of production. Many had technical training, and if they had degrees, they tended to be from state universities or engineering schools. They were mobile, middle-class Republicans who married suffragette wives, practiced liberal religions like Unitarianism or Christian Science, and were passionately interested in music. They were self-made men with considerable money to spend on a house but few preconceptions as to what it should look like, and they lacked great collections of art or heirlooms that would have to be accommodated in their new houses. As a group they stand in marked contrast to the upper-class, North Shore establishment that patronized revivalist architects like Howard Van Doren Shaw. These men represented second or third generation wealth. They were East Coast educated, often with degrees from Ivy League schools. They were high level executives, salesmen, and financiers, who belonged to five or six Chicago clubs, were Episcopalians, collected antiques, and seldom married suffragette women. They often patronized the orchestra but seldom played instruments or sang themselves. They were not the inventor type, and they tended to look upon culture as something to be imported.

Robie approached Wright around Christmas 1906. He had done some sketches of the kind of house he wanted, probably simple diagrams showing the arrangement of rooms, and when he showed them to contractors and architects he kept getting the reply, "I know what you want, one of those damn Wright houses."[10] We do not know where the preliminary contacts were made, but if they followed the usual pattern, the two men would eventually have met in the library of Wright's Oak Park studio. The setting can be reconstructed.[11] This little octagonal room, originally built in 1898 to house a free circulating library of books on the fine arts, soon became a reception room for Wright's prospective clients, a tiny baptistery where they were initiated into the mysteries of the prairie house (fig. 7). Contemporary photographs show it cluttered with Wrightian furniture and arrangements of dried flowers, but also with piles of photographs of Wright's buildings on the table, and framed presentation drawings mounted to swing out from the wall for the browser's convenience, with tracing paper plans loosely mounted on top of them. It was here that the full range of Wright's style could be shown, the client's wallet opened, and reluctant spouses won over. When in 1910 Wright had the first of his so-called Wasmuth volumes published in Germany, with its colored drawings on heavy paper alternating with light tissue-paper plans, it was surely an attempt to open up

Figure 7. Frank Lloyd Wright Studio, Oak Park, interior of library (Wasmuth 1911)

the Oak Park library to a wider world and to evoke in a European audience the thrill that patrons of Robie's generation had felt in browsing through the Oak Park drawings.[12]

In his reminiscences of 1958, Robie claimed that he went to Wright knowing exactly the kind of house he wanted: "no junk" in the way of shades or curtains; maximum sunlight, with shading provided only by broad overhanging eaves; separate nursery facilities; a yard with a wall to keep the children in and kidnappers out; rooms without interruptions; and a view out over his neighbors without relinquishing any of his privacy. On the surface it sounds as if he could have designed the house without Wright.

The problem with his account, however, is that it is colored not only by having lived in the house but also by having read Wright's *Autobiography* of 1932.[13] It might be safer to assume that Robie did not know quite so specifically what he wanted, that aside from rejecting some conventions, the positive side of his program was, as he himself said in 1958, "so nebulous that I could not explain it to anybody."[14] Probably Wright sensed that he was a man waiting to be educated, willing to come halfway or more toward the architect's ideals: "But the man who loves the beautiful, with ideals of organic natures of an artist, is too keenly sensible of the nature of his client as a fundamental condition of his problem to cast him off, although he may give him something to grow to, something in which he may be a little ill at ease at the outset."[15] Wright's metaphor for the architect-client relationship was the relationship between the portrait painter and the sitter: "Is a portrait, say by Sargent, any less a revelation of the character of the subject because it bears his stamp and is easily recognized as a Sargent? Does one lose individuality when interpreted sympathetically by one of his own race and time who can know him and his needs intimately and idealize them?"[16] Obviously not. The architect does not, in Wright's view, lose sight of the client's character, but Wright does tend to idealize him and his tastes. Wright had already begun to think of himself as the voice of those who could not speak for themselves, as the fulfillment of Sullivan's image of the artist embodying the deepest ideals of his age, above and beyond the needs of a specific client: "The clairvoyance of the age is steadily unfolding and it will result therefrom that the greatest poet will be he who shall grasp and deify the commonplace of our life, those simple, normal feelings which the people of this day will be helpless otherwise to express."[17] As Wright looked over Robie's crude sketches, this idealizing process must already have begun. By the time Robie's "portrait" was finished four years later, it would evoke the artist much more vividly than the sitter.

DESCRIPTION OF THE ROBIE HOUSE

Before turning to the house as it stands today, it is interesting to study it under construction, which can be done thanks to a series of about thirty photographs taken by the contractor in 1909–10.[18] Even the small selection reproduced here allows us to see the building slowly rise from the empty lot, and to appreciate something of its extraordinary technology. Figure 8 is taken from 58th Street looking northeast, with the front porch of the neighboring house on Woodlawn Avenue shown on the extreme left. (This house was demolished and replaced by a modern dormitory belonging to the Chicago Theological Seminary in about 1960.) Teams of horses stand ready with what look like plows but are probably scoops used to dig out shallow foundation trenches. They remind us that, beyond a shallow excavation for the boiler, there is no cellar under the Robie House, and that, as in other Wright houses, functions normally assigned to basements are here carried on above ground. Figures 9–14 illustrate the structure in the making. The vertical piers are solid brick, while the horizontal members are large, bolted steel beams. The technology is different from that of skyscraper construction, where revetted metal beams, were used for both horizontal and vertical members. But the photographs show

Figure 8. Site of Robie House, 1909 (H. B. Barnard Co.)

Figure 9. Robie House in construction, 1909 (H. B. Barnard Co.)

Figure 10. Robie House in construction, looking southwest towards the University of Chicago, 1909 (H. B. Barnard Co.)

Figure 11. Robie house in construction, 1909 (H. B. Barnard Co.)

Figure 12. Robie House in construction, garage wing, 1909 (H. B. Barnard Co.)

Figure 13. Robie House in construction, 1909 (H. B. Barnard Co.)

Figure 14. Robie House in construction, 1909 (H. B. Barnard Co.)

Figure 15. Fricke-Martin House, Oak Park, by Frank Lloyd Wright, 1901, altered 1907.

that there is much more steel in the house than is usually supposed, a fact that can be corroborated today by a look under the long south balcony or through the wooden grilles in the living room ceiling. Figure 5 also shows the Robies as a prosperous couple posing with their young son.[19] Figure 11 shows the main body of the house in construction, with the brick jambs that will eventually hold the twelve French doors of the living room and dining room. The long south balcony has been begun, but the parapet has been temporarily left unfinished, probably to ease the job of raising materials to the upper parts of the house. Figure 10 shows the floor of what seems to be the top story, taken from the rear of the house looking southwest toward the site of the fledgling University of Chicago, Mrs. Robie's alma mater.[20] Another photograph (fig. 12) shows the garage wing nearing completion. The so-called stern of the house is visible at the left, with the skeleton of the cantilevered roof above it and the framework of the master bedroom wing at the top. The photograph gives a good idea of the enormous amount of wood in what must be a very flammable building. Figure 13 shows the house, now nearing completion, from the classic diagonal viewpoint near the crossing of 58th Street and Woodlawn. The main story is completed and roofed, while the master bedroom wing is still in construction. The chimney is shown as an odd combination of two separate structures: a broad, flat mass of brick on the right and an appendage on the left which, at this stage, resembles a large wooden box. Only after the final cladding of brick will these two pieces fuse into the L-shaped chimney of the finished house. Figure 14 shows the house nearly complete in structure but still without its complement of doors and windows. The driveway is sealed by a high wall (which was lowered in a restoration in the 1960s), and a massive brick wall protrudes along the back alley to the sidewalk and the very limits of the property. The final photograph (cover illustration) shows the house complete and gives a good idea of the setting, including the broad stretch of empty land in the foreground extending as far south as the Midway. It also shows the comparatively great height of the neighboring houses that loom, with quaint turrets and huge attic dormers, over Wright's severe, low, and level roof.

It is time to take a close look at the house as it stands today.

Like many of Wright's mature houses, it looks extremely complicated as a total composition, but it can be broken down visually into simpler parts. It follows what might be called the law of interlocking masses.[21] This principle is shown at work even more clearly in a building like the Fricke-Martin House in Oak Park, built in 1901 but altered in 1907 (fig. 15).[22] Each large component of the house is designed in strict symmetry, but the components are allowed to combine in a fluid way. It is as though the laws of physics had been momentarily suspended so that one solid mass could interpenetrate another until at a certain point these laws were suddenly reasserted and the drifting masses locked into place. At the Robie House one of these interlocking masses can be found by looking at the master bedroom wing on the uppermost story (fig. 16). It follows a T-shaped plan, and left to itself it would have been almost completely symmetrical. But it was allowed to interpenetrate another large component, the two stories that sit underneath the long cantilevered roof. The bedroom looks as though it drifted into the roof below it and fit snugly behind the chimney before being frozen into place. Should it ever drift away again, the long roof and everything below it would return to absolute axial symmetry. In fact, it is interesting to take a broadside view of the house and test the strictness of this symmetry (fig. 17). It turns out to be a key to the design. The two giant flower urns obviously balance one another, but so do the piers on which they stand, the piers on which the long balcony seems to rest, and even the clusters of piers that hold up the roof. At first glance there seems to be only one small discrepancy, the absence of any counterweight to the front porch at the rear of the house. But old photographs show that this flaw is the result of a recent restoration[23] and that the driveway wall originally stood as high as the front porch, acting as its pendant.

Wright's commitment to symmetry in the design of the individual components of the house has two sources, the formal planning of the École des Beaux-Arts and Friedrich Froebel's philosophy of kindergarten education. As Hitchcock has shown in a classic study, Wright had turned himself into the ablest academic designer in Chicago in the early 1890s, purely through autodidactic effort, assimilating the lessons of the École indirectly through European periodicals and through contact with the work of Bruce

Figure 16. Robie House, bedroom wing (Richard Nickel)

Figure 17. South side of Robie House
     above: west end (Margaret Olin)
     opposite: east end (Margaret Olin)

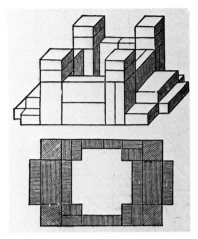

Figure 18. Froebel gifts (M. Kraus-Boelte, *The Kindergarten Guide*, 1881)

Price and McKim, Mead, and White.[24] He toyed with occasional classicizing motifs, but more importantly, he developed such ingrained habits of design as axial symmetry of plan and elevation and the expression of interior spaces on exterior massing. A building like the Blossom House of 1892 in Hyde Park cannot be understood apart from either its specific model (the now-demolished Taylor House in Newport, built by McKim, Mead, and White in 1885–86),[25] or the classical principles of symmetry and massing on which it is designed.

On the other hand, the Blossom House also shows an interest in simple, block-like masses that came to Wright from Froebel's kindergarten "gifts." In Froebel's system, after an introduction stressing music, dance, colors, and textures, the child-craftsman was taught to manipulate blocks and squares, and later lines and circles, into patterns and constructions that Froebel called the "forms of life," the "forms of beauty," and the "forms of knowledge" (fig. 18). In other words, he was taught a kind of rule-governed play that had symbolic overtones about the kinds of order present in nature and in the universe at large. The forms of life were familiar objects from everyday experience, such as armchairs, shops, engines, bridges, clocks, and on a more architectural level, gates, churches, monuments, stables, houses, and triumphal arches. But on a still higher and more abstract level were the forms of beauty, symmetrical arrangements of blocks in which the child had to "keep the opposites alike," since nature herself followed laws, and "a lopsided form is no more beautiful than a lopsided tree." When a child manipulated the blocks through all possible orderly permutations, he then attained the forms of knowledge.[26] Wright claimed that his mother introduced him to Froebel's gifts in 1876, when he was a child of nine in a Boston suburb, and that the lessons he learned never left him. "The smooth shapely maple blocks with which to build, the sense of which never afterward leaves the fingers: so *form* became *feeling*."[27] But of equal importance was Wright's mature rediscovery of Froebel when he was about twenty-five, and when his wife was active as a kindergarten teacher in Oak Park.[28] The influence of the blocks can be seen in the Blossom House of 1892, and the influence of other Froebel patterns in the Romeo and Juliet Windmill of 1897 in Spring Green.[29] Louis Sullivan's rejection of

Figure 19. Robie House, connection between east end and the garage wing (Margaret Olin)

Figure 20. Robie House, view from the north (Margaret Olin)

formal education and his rhapsodic linkage of childhood and nature—for example, in his essay of 1896 contrasting "emotional" and "classical" architecture—reinforced a direction in which Wright was already headed.[30] By the time of the Larkin Building and Unity Temple (1904–5), Wright had turned to Froebel as his chief source for a new, self-conscious primitivism in exterior design.

On returning to the Robie House, one discovers that Wright could shape the exterior of a building with colossal Froebel blocks, but then, when he wanted, make one forget the whole Froebel system with a few brilliant psychological tricks. For instance, the garage wing that stands at the rear of the house could not possibly have a pendant on the opposite side. There was no need for one and no space. So Wright cleverly detaches the garage from the main house, not physically but perceptually (fig. 19). Just at the point where the garage roof and the roof of the main house should merge, Wright opens up a long, narrow slit that separates them again at least in a visual sense. Just beneath the slit there is a grid of posts and lintels, which lines up with the windows on both the south and north side of the kitchen[31] and acts like a series of perforations, allowing the eye to pull the whole garage wing apart with just a gentle tug.

When one looks for perceptual tricks of this sort, one finds that the Robie House is full of them. Wright's reputation as a great innovator in the realm of structure has obscured the fact that he was also a brilliant visual psychologist. For example, the long balcony that runs along the side of the house is in fact supported by metal beams that protrude at regular intervals from the living and dining room floors. But with the stone copings above and below, the balcony itself looks like one giant I-beam, supported by a great brick post at either end. It functions as a metaphor for an old-fashioned system of support, post and lintel construction, next to which the bold cantilever of the roof appears all that much more bold and soaring. On the north side of the house, where there is no balcony, the same cantilevered roof looks slightly tamer (fig. 20). In bright sunlight the balcony casts a broad band of shadow and reinforces the horizontal lines of the design. But so does the very texture of the brickwork (fig. 21). Wright not only used the famous long Roman brick, but had the masons conceal all the vertical joints while all horizontal joints were deeply un-

Figure 21. Robie House, detail of brickwork (Margaret Olin)

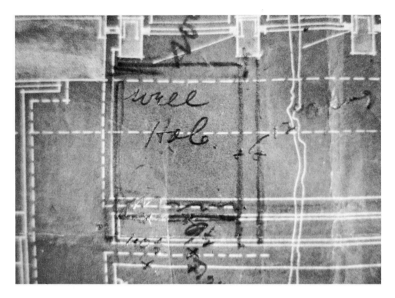

derscored.[32] The result is (or was before insensitive restoration in many places) a corduroy effect that acts on the spectator below the obvious thresholds of perception, reinforcing the dominant horizontal lines.

Even while the house was in construction, Wright kept alert for further opportunities of this kind. The original plans called for fourteen French doors that would open out onto the balcony from the living and dining rooms. But as the metal beams of the balcony were being bolted into place, Wright must have felt that he could exploit still further the skeletal possibilities of iron and steel construction. He took the contractor's copy of the blueprints and opened up a well or pit at each end of the balcony (fig. 22), and at the same time, to avoid the obvious danger of anyone falling through these pits, he changed the first and the fourteenth doors into windows. From the street these changes are hard to detect, but to anyone looking up through these hatches to the roofs flying above them, the effect is intensely dramatic (fig. 23), and the house begins to take on some of the freedom and romance of advanced nautical design.

Perhaps the most interesting manipulation of perception occurs in the way the Robie House occupies its site.[33] The 60-foot lot

Figure 23. Robie House, view up
through well-hole of balcony (Margaret
Olin)

that Robie purchased in 1906 is the narrowest lot on this stretch
of Woodlawn Avenue. Old photographs of the next house to the
north (on the left of fig. 8) show that it had a front porch facing
south, which seems to indicate that it originally enjoyed a view
south as far as the Midway and that its owner sold Robie a narrow
strip of his own front lawn. If so, this would explain why Robie
was under a verbal obligation to build a house worth at least
$20,000,[34] although in the end he had in fact spent much more.
Despite its expense, however, the new building was the most
unneighborly of houses. It turned a bare brick wall to its neighbor
on the north. Its design included boundary walls that ran to the
very edges of the lot on the north and east, jealously staking out

27

the property and standing in contrast to the shared lawns and spirit of mutual trust that characterize the older houses in the area. But it is the narrow front on Woodlawn Avenue that shows Wright at his most aggressive. All of the older houses on the street are set back 38 feet from the property line. To judge from the other houses, however, the setback code seems to have permitted a few minor infringements as a matter of course. Up and down the street broad eaves overhang the setback line, small porches protrude in front of it, and bay windows bulge out into the space reserved for lawns (fig. 24). We do not know whether these rules derive from a zoning law or whether they were embodied in informal neighborly agreements, but every house on Woodlawn Avenue observes them. Even the Robie House does, although it hardly looks set back (figs. 17, 20 and front cover). Wright obeyed the letter of the law, but violated its spirit. His cantilevered roof and front porch protrude to such an abnormal extent and, together with the pointed bay window, are such integral parts of the design, that the whole Robie House seems to extend almost to the sidewalk, unconfined by neighborly rules, the one outlaw on an otherwise restrained and law-abiding street.

Once the house has shouldered its way in among its more stately neighbors, it relaxes and presents a remarkably open face to the two corner streets. In this respect it is just the opposite of H. H. Richardson's Glessner House, built on a similar corner lot at Prairie Avenue and 18th Street in 1886.[35] Glessner House is a medieval fortress, with a rugged outside wall protecting a hidden garden, with meandering lanes, in the Olmstead fashion, on the inside. The Robie House fends off intrusion in much more civilized ways, by hiding the entrances and making visitors follow complicated, twisting paths to get inside. It also puts its gardens on public display. The two giant urns, as well as the stone copings along the front of the porch and along the entire length of the balcony and the master bedroom wing, were filled with planters so that the house could "blossom with the season" and appear "married to the ground."[36] Wright conceived of the severe and blocky forms of these houses as a conventionalized foil for nature, and his rendering in the Wasmuth portfolio of 1910 shows the house smothered in foliage.[37] The photograph in the 1911 Wasmuth volume was doctored to make the trees planted along the

Figure 24. Houses on Woodlawn Avenue between 57th and 58th Streets (Margaret Olin)

sidewalk look as though they were actually growing out of the small flower garden between the two urns.[38] Like the famous tree that Wright left growing through the eaves of the Winslow stables,[39] these plantings, or apparent plantings, would have given a patina of age to the Robie House, as though the house and plantings had grown up together over the years:

> You do not feel that these buildings have been dropped accidentally upon the ground or into holes dug carelessly. The artificial structure reaches out and fraternizes with the natural environment, inviting flower and vine in turn to clamber over walls and flourish within curb of brick and stone, each mingling with each. . . . There is no painfully hard and fast line between nature and art.[40]

Getting into the Robie House is no easy matter, since the doors are located in out of the way places. The garage wing and the children's playlot in front of it were originally protected by a high brick wall (fig. 14). Wright first designed a sliding wooden grille for the driveway entrance, but later substituted a pair of swinging iron gates, forged in the same pattern as the leaded windows.[41] There were three entrances to the house from the driveway area. One led into the children's playroom on the ground floor, and another to the laundry and furnace room on the same level. A modern storm door and windowed panel installed at the edge of the building now conceal the fact that one used to walk deep in under the shelter of the house before encountering the doors. The third entrance was set even deeper and was reached by mounting the servants' staircase and knocking at the kitchen door on the second story. The views through the open brick grid (fig. 19) would have provided a dash of drama for the iceman climbing up to the icebox at the top of the stairs.[42] It is also possible to walk from the driveway through the garden on the long side of the house and to enter the billiard room through four adjacent doors, or to keep going to the west end of the balcony and climb the stairs that lead up to the front porch. The porch is not very high, but the stairs are narrow and the visitor is forced close up against massive blocks of brick, so much so that the simple act of ascending is turned into an intense experience, something like scaling the face of a cliff, complete with the reward of interesting views back down from the summit. From the porch it is possible

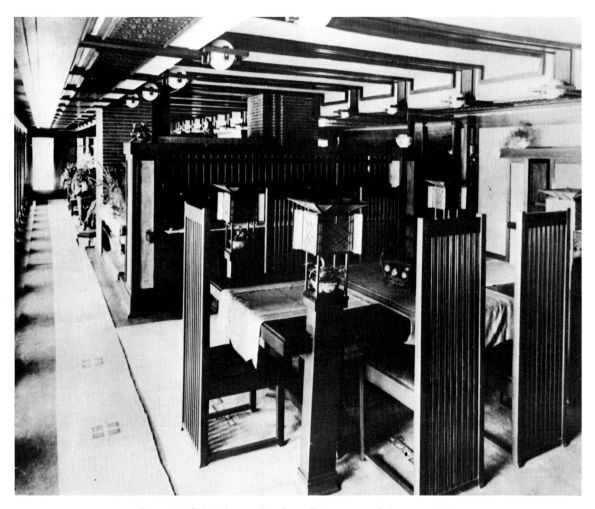

Figure 25. Robie House, view from dining room to living room, 1917, during the occupancy of Marshall D. Wilber (Wilbert Hasbrouck)

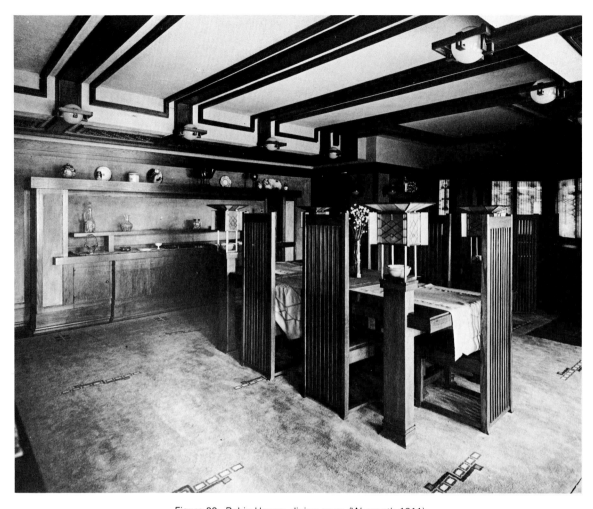

Figure 26. Robie House, dining room (Wasmuth 1911)

Figure 27. Robie House, dining room, 1917, during the occupancy of Marshall D. Wilber (Wilbert Hasbrouck)

Figure 28. Robie House, living room with fireplace (Margaret Olin)

Figure 29. Robie House, west end of living room with a copy of the original sofa (Margaret Olin)

to enter directly into the living room through two glass doors, or to descend to the ground again and head for the main door. Here at last is the principle entrance to the house, tucked away on the north side of the building and hidden beneath the low clearance of the guest room balcony. The entrance itself, now two doors, was originally a single oak door with a large art-glass window in the center.[43]

Inside the entrance there is a small reception room and then the two main areas of the ground floor, the billiard room and the children's playroom. Both are low and dark, and Wright himself thought of them as basement rooms even though they stand above ground.[44] Guests would ordinarily overlook them and ascend directly to the ceremonial and entertainment rooms of the upper story. The staircase is a well that leads from dark to light. Originally there was a slatted screen that shielded it for a moment from the dining area and increased the feeling of surprise that a guest must have felt on reaching the top. What awaited the visitor was one of the great breathtaking spaces of American domestic architecture (fig. 25). Instead of a conventional room, one entered a much more fluid kind of space, where the boundaries were not solid walls but thin wooden screens, curtains, and an extraordinary number of glass doors and windows. The removal of the screens and curtains in later restorations has made the space more starkly open than Wright would have wanted,[45] but in any case what is happening is that spaces and functions normally kept separate are conjoined. In Wright's earliest houses the traditional front and back parlor had already been merged into a single living room through "the removal of an already half-eliminated partition."[46] But in the Robie House the living room is fused with the dining room as well, which contains in turn the vestiges of still another independent space, the breakfast nook set into the east bay window to catch the sunrise. The fireplace, which should serve as an anchor and close off any normal room, is here treated like a heavy but, in a sense, still moveable piece of furniture. At the top it is reduced to two slender piers of brick, and everything that suggests the flow of space—moldings, light fixtures, rugs, balcony doors—drifts calmly past or through it. Fire is reduced to the realm of pure symbol,[47] and no matter how brightly the logs set on Wright's geometrical andirons might burn, the room is heated by an efficient modern system of sunken or hidden radiators and lit by numerous electric fixtures.[48]

As spaces became joined and traditional boundaries vanished, a new kind of furniture moved in to take the place of walls and other partitions by setting up barriers where they would be most missed. This was the function of the famous dining room set, which although once severely altered, has now been reconstructed and is on display in the David and Alfred Smart Gallery of the University of Chicago. In its original position the set served to create a room within a room (fig. 26).[49] The high backs concealed guests from servants, while the lamposts prevented attention from leaking away at the corners. The furniture contributed to an extraordinary sense of intimacy across the table, and one can easily imagine it steering the guests toward a single, unified conversation and away from fragmented chatter. The Robies used it only on formal occasions and preferred to dine by themselves at the small square table in the breakfast nook, but even that had the same high-backed chairs and must have offered the same sense of intimacy, though on a smaller scale. It is usually assumed that the living room represents a less controlled environment, designed for a period of relaxed and less ritualized entertainment following a formal dinner party. From what we can tell from old photographs, furniture was used in it to give a loose definition to separate functions. A desk and custom-made lamp created a kind of study (fig. 30). A permanent bench with a slatted screen defined a space on one side of the hearth, while moveable furniture was arranged on the other side to create an informal inglenook.[50]

There are few better examples than the Robie House of what Wright meant by constitutional ornament:

> In the main the ornamentation is wrought in the warp and woof of the structure. It is constitutional in the best sense and is felt in the conception of the ground plan. To elucidate this element in composition would mean a long story and perhaps a tedious one though to me it is the most fascinating phase of the work, involving the true poetry of conception.[51]

In his best interiors, a kind of polyphony is set up between the small details of ornament and larger themes of space and structure. The built-in sideboard of the dining room (fig. 27) echoes the

exterior of the house with its juxtaposition of cantilever and old-fashioned post and lintel structure. The pattern of the leading in the windows can be read in several ways—for example, as an abstract flower or as something like a Japanese lantern flattened into two dimensions—but the diamond pattern also echoes the pointed shapes introduced into the plan by the bay windows at either end of the house. The patterns of the leading on the balcony doors stop halfway down, first because this creates the illusion of symmetry with the windows opposite them, and second because the occupants' privacy needed protection only at the top. The balcony shielded the bottom of the doors from the gaze of any passerby. The ceiling of the living and dining rooms follows a shape dictated by the structure (figs. 28 and 29). It is relatively low at the sides, where a pair of welded-steel channel beams runs along the entire length of the house, but it rises at the center, exploiting some of the dead space under the peak of the roof. Wooden grilles of a beautifully abstract pattern provide ventilation and allow a gentle kind of indirect lighting from hidden bulbs under the roof beams. Moldings bring the ceiling alive by turning corners at the most unexpected places, as though to flaunt their independence of the surfaces to which they are attached. The main lights that run down the entire length of both rooms are made out of glass globes of a common, mass-produced sort, but they are held in place by ingenious wooden frames that suggest the kind of delicacy needed to catch and hold a bubble.

If the large fused spaces of these ceremonial rooms strikes the modern visitor as an extravagance, we should not forget that the Robie House is a very big place with plenty of private rooms. In addition to the three ground-floor rooms and the open spaces just discussed, there is a kitchen with its pantries, a servants' dining room, two maid's rooms, four main bedrooms, and six bathrooms, not to mention the laundry, furnace room, wine cellar, eleven closets, and a three-car garage. Each of the four bedrooms looks out over a ledge of foliage growing from urns or planters. The master bedroom has its own fireplace, bath, dressing room with ingenious linen drawers that slide back into the space beneath the windows and the planters, and finally a walk-in closet, where there is a safe built into the side of the chimney and a door leading to a small private balcony (figs. 44 and 45).

It is, in fact, a very well-appointed house, which is why Robie paid so much for it. Payments recorded in the contractor's account book between 15 April 1909 and 21 June 1910 total $26,516.19, but these reflect only part of the expenses and would have excluded the furnishings, since they were entrusted to the firm of Niedecken-Walbridge in Milwaukee.[52] In 1958 Robie recalled that he had spent $14,000 for the lot, $35,000 for the house, and $10,000 for the furnishings, coming to a total of $59,000.[53] Compared to the $4,700 that the young Wright spent on his own house in 1889, or even to the $20,000 spent on both the Winslow House in 1893 and the Ward Willits House in 1902–3, it was an expensive house.[54]

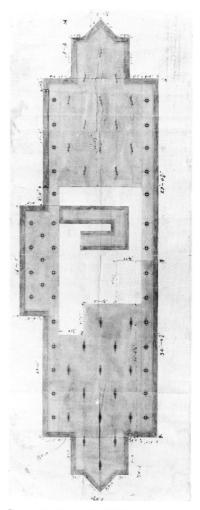

Figure 31. Frank Lloyd Wright, architect, and George M. Niedecken, delineator, design for the rugs of the living and dining rooms of the Robie House, 1910 (Collection Prairie Archives, Milwaukee Art Museum)

39

□ □ □ □ DESIGN OF □ □ □ □
THE ROBIE HOUSE

Describing the Robie House as it stands is not the same as showing how it was designed. What exactly did Wright do when Robie came to him with his crude sketches in late 1906? The question raises the broader problem of how Wright went about designing any building. For all of the voluminous literature on the architect, this fundamental question is seldom raised. Wright himself opens up the pages of this closed book only once, in the part of his *Autobiography* where he tells how Unity Temple was designed in 1904. Although written 28 years after the event, it still remains the best glimpse we have over the shoulder of the architect at work.

The design began to crystallize not on paper but in his mind: "Imagination conceives here the PLAN suitable to the material and the purpose of the whole, seeing the probable possible form clearer all the time."[55] A sheet of blank paper stood ready on the drawing board, and as the evening lengthened, Wright approached it with a sense of mounting excitement: "A thrilling moment in any architect's experience. He is about to see the countenance of something he is invoking with intense concentration." By dawn Wright had completed three related diagrams: "the plan, section and elevation in the main. . . . There is no 'sketch' and there never has been one. There seldom is in a thought-built building."

By "sketch" Wright means more picturesque methods of design, such as those of his early employer, Joseph Lyman Silsbee: "Silsbee got a ground-plan and made his pretty sketch, getting some charming picturesque effect he had in mind. Then the sketch would come out into the drawing room to be fixed up into a building, keeping the floor plan near the sketch if possible. . . . The picture interests him. The rest bores him."[56] In contrast to Silsbee, Wright worked out a process of design that was highly cerebral and abstract, one committed in advance to rules of symmetry and to an experimental attitude toward mass and space, but concerned rather less with the outward look of the final building. If problems had to be worked out, they were likely to be cerebral problems of proportion, balance, harmony—just the kind of thing that would concern a classical architect. For example, there were difficulties establishing harmony between Unity Temple and Unity House: "Thirty-four studies were necessary to arrive at this concordance as it is now seen. Unfortunately the studies are lost with thousands of others of many other buildings. . . . I wish I had kept them. Unity House looks easy enough now, for it is right enough. But it was not."[57]

But once these relationships had been worked out, the look of the building would take care of itself. There are several splendid perspective renderings of Unity Temple, for instance the drawing later printed in the Wasmuth portfolio of 1910, but these came after the design was completed and were concerned with presenting the building rather than shaping it.[58] The same is true of many of the early houses, the Charnley House of 1891, for instance, or the Blossom House of 1892, which were designed according to strict codes of symmetry and ignore the possibilities of their corner sites with a certain cool aloofness. When Wright talks about the abstractness of design, we get a glimpse of the child looking down over an array of Froebel blocks sitting on a grid, or the beaux-arts architect working out his plan with a certain grand detachment unavailable to the ordinary spectator, who sees only one part of the building at a time and whose view is conditioned by the site. Structures like the Larkin Building were first

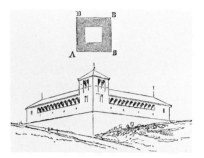

Figure 32. Viollet-le-Duc, plan of a fortress (*Discourses on Architecture*, 1875)

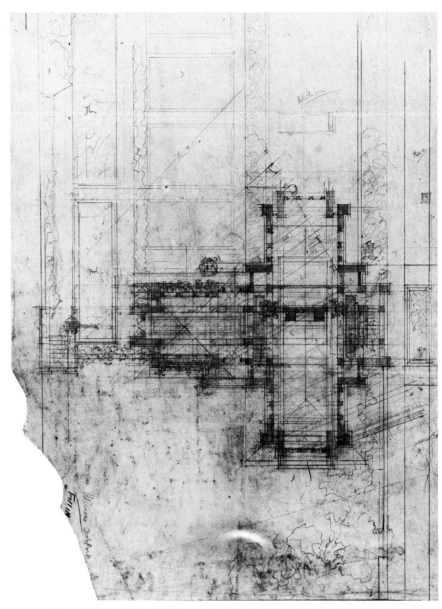

Figure 33. Frank Lloyd Wright, project for the Ullman House, Oak Park, 1904
(© 1959 The Frank Lloyd Wright Foundation)

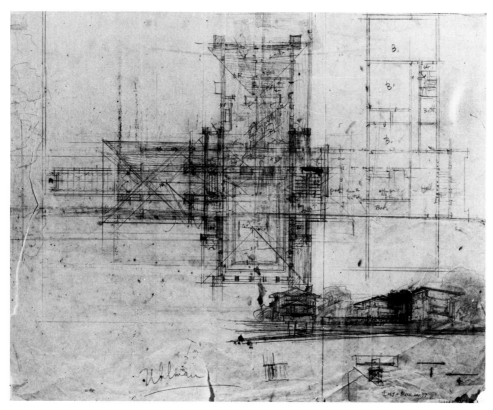

Figure 34. Frank Lloyd Wright, plan and perspective proof of the Ullman House, 1904
(© 1955 The Frank Lloyd Wright Foundation)

designed in symmetry and only later shown in perspective. Although the perspective renderings are images of great dramatic power, they appear late in the process of design:

> The schemes are conceived in three dimensions as organic entities, let the picturesque perspective fall how it will. While a sense of the incidental perspectives the design will develop is always present, I have great faith that if the thing is rightly put together in true organic sense with proportions actually right the picturesque will take care of itself. No man ever built a building worthy of the name of architecture who fashioned it in perspective sketch to his taste and then fudged the plan to suit. Such methods produce mere scene-painting. A perspective may be a proof but it is no nurture.[59]

And yet, in the years just before the Robie House, Wright's system does bend to accommodate the spectator's way of seeing, and one of the most fascinating developments in his growth is the way perspective works its way under the skin of his buildings in these years. One factor was the influence of Viollet-le-Duc. This great French medievalist and architect developed a cogent critique of abstract systems of planning in his *Discourses on Architecture,* which Wright studied in Henry Van Brunt's translation of 1875.[60] Viollet-le-Duc respected formal planning but placed even greater stress on the requirements of the eye. Buildings are seen from ground level and their view is determined by the conditions of approach. They should be planned not according to such purely mechanical laws as symmetry, but according to such artistic laws as harmony and balance: "Balance is not symmetry, as it admits of variety." To illustrate his point he gives the example of a square fortress set on a hilltop with the ground falling off sharply to one side (fig. 32). The program calls for a tower. While symmetry would dictate placing the tower in the center of one of the wings, balance dictates a corner position, since "the eye requires that the extra story shall be placed where the character of the site renders the greatest solidity and strength necessary." By insisting on the requirements of the eye, Viollet-le-Duc paved the way for a reentry of the picturesque into formal design, although it was a new, disciplined, mathematical version of the picturesque, a world apart from what Wright would call "mere scene-painting."

The key to this new development in Wright's work is the concept of the "perspective proof." ("Perspective may be a proof but it is no nurture.'') As the architect worked on the interlocking diagram (plan with section or elevation attached) in front of him, he might not have an entirely clear idea of what the building would look like. To fill in this blind spot, he would construct a small perspective sketch. Like a printmaker who works for hours on a plate before he finally pulls a proof to see where the image is going, and who studies the result with a certain amount of surprise, the architect ''pulls'' a perspective-proof of the building to see what it will really look like, and then returns to his interlocking diagram to register corrections and revisions. One example, slightly earlier than the Robie House, brings us as close as we will probably ever come to the way Wright worked. It is a plan of 1904 for the Ullman House in Oak Park.[61] Smudged and messy, full of changes, it belongs to the fluid stage when a design is still evolving (fig. 33). It shows a T-shaped plan originally laid out in a strict axial symmetry. Every Froebel block has its pendant, and every shift or erasure on one side of the plan is balanced by a similar move on the other side. At a certain point, however, Wright apparently felt the need to see more vividly where the design was going. He covered the drawing with a series of radiant lines that all stem from the same point off the lower left corner of the sheet. Like rays of vision, these lines intersect the plan in such a way as to indicate how the house would appear to a single spectator. One might say that the plan is strafed from a vantage point outside it. The lines were used to construct a perspective proof taken from just this position (fig. 34). The proof told Wright that the requirements of the eye were not being entirely met. Accordingly, the plan was pulled and stretched so that in its final version the house would present a more impressive appearance to the viewer, and indeed this is exactly what the final design in the Wasmuth portfolio shows (fig. 35). This is not the same as Silsbee's method, where the picture of the house came first and the plan was ''fudged to suit,'' but it does represent a rare marriage between an abstract system of design and the requirements of the eye.[62] It was just this marriage that would produce the Robie House.

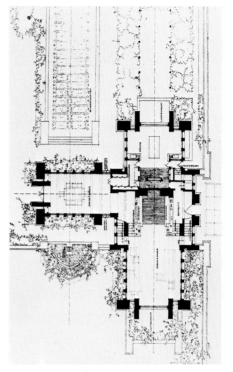

Figure 35. Ullman House, final plan (Wasmuth 1910)

□ □ THE ROBIE SEQUENCE □ □
ROBIE 1-4

When an architectural historian wants to reconstruct the genesis of a design, he normally looks for the early drawings and tries to establish their sequence. Sketches and working drawings are what really count, since they show the ideas in flux. The problem with the Robie House is that no such drawings have yet come to light. Either Wright threw them out (as the remarks about Unity Temple quoted above seem to imply) or they were lost in the Taliesin fire of 1914. What we have are the contractor's blueprints, several measured studies for furniture and interior details, and a couple of perspective renderings[63]—all interesting, but totally unrevealing about the way the design came into being. To catch a glimpse of the house in the making we must approach the problem in an unconventional way. Wright worked by type, building up what he called "a constantly accumulating residue of formula."[64] Thus it is possible to single out a few earlier examples of the Robie type and to treat them like preliminary drawings. In fact the Robie House turns out to be the fourth time Wright resorted to the same basic formula, and the three previous buildings—which can conveniently be labelled Robie 1 to Robie 3—shed great light on the final Robie design.

Figure 36. Frank Lloyd Wright, project for the Yahara Boat Club, Madison,. 1902 (Wasmuth 1910)

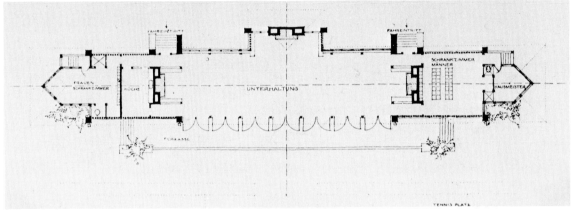

Figure 37. River Forest Tennis Club, by Frank Lloyd Wright, 1906 (Wasmuth 1911)

Figure 38. Tomek House, Riverside, by Frank Lloyd Wright, 1907 (Wasmuth 1911)

Figure 39. Tomek House (Wasmuth 1911)

Figure 40. Tomek House, living room with fireplace (Margaret Olin)

Robie 1 is an unexecuted design of 1902 for the Yahara Boat Club in Madison (fig. 36).[65] Obviously the program was different from that of a house—clubhouse on the upper floor and storage space for racing sculls on the lower level—but the exterior form is like a simple, narrow prairie house. The design is totally symmetrical and gives the appearance (for the most part fictitious) of being built up out of Froebel blocks. There is no concession whatsoever to picturesque perspective.

Robie 2 is the River Forest Tennis Club of 1906 (fig. 37).[66] It is still completely symmetrical, but the number of Froebel blocks has increased and they are arranged in more complex patterns. Now there is a long cantilevered roof at either end of the building and pointed bay windows underneath. There is a terrace onto which several pairs of doors open, anticipating the Robie House balcony, and the walls are built with a board and batten construction that tends to emphasize the horizontal lines, as does the corduroy effect of the Robie House bricks.

Robie 3, the Tomek House of 1907 in Riverside, is the same idea elaborated still further (figs. 38 and 39).[67] In retrospect, it looks almost like a trial run for the famous Robie 4. The long cantilevered roof is supported by dense clusters of Froebel blocks arranged as mirror reflections of one another. The symmetry would have been still more apparent if a garden wall had been built on the left, as planned, to act as the pendant to the porch on the right. Unlike either of its predecessors, the Tomek House follows the so-called law of intersecting masses. The bedroom wing on the top story has been allowed to drift in behind the chimney and intersect the main roof before being locked into place. This wing gives the house the same kind of balance that one finds in a ship with a bridge placed at one end of the deck. It also provides a sense of forward motion that was missing in the simple symmetries of Robie 1 and 2, and the front porch suggests that the house has pulled into a berth. The entrance is marked by a cluster of "blocks" and a door leading directly to a staircase that rises in a single flight behind the chimney. As one mounts the stairs one ascends into a brilliant box of glass that allows the visitor to see into the dining room, but also serves to protect the interior from cold blasts from outside. As might be intuited from the long ribbon of windows on the exterior, there is a dramatic flow of space

Figure 41. Tomek House, detail of interior (Margaret Olin)

from the living room to the dining room, a flow emphasized by the simple wooden moldings that follow the lines of the long steel beams hidden in the ceiling (fig. 40). At key points the moldings pass over smaller beams that jump across the space like little bridges, suggesting boundaries but allowing the eye to penetrate beyond (fig. 41). The flow of space exists on only one side of the fireplace, however. On the other side there is no direct link between the two rooms, but rather access to a staircase heading for the upper story. The dining room is narrower and more intimate than the living room and is illuminated from above by artificial light shining down through art-glass panels inserted into the ceiling. A little further on is the breakfast nook, smaller and more intimate still, with a ceiling of glass blocks set in concrete that allows daylight to shine in from the outdoor balcony above.

Robie 4, the Robie House itself, is a proven formula rethought in the context of a new site and a more lavish patron. The clusters of Froebel blocks are the most complicated yet, and the composition is made even more complex by the flower urns and outlying walls around the garden and driveway (fig. 17). The bedroom wing is more elaborate, and the feeling of movement from front to back, one might say from stern to prow, is more pronounced. Instead of the plain stucco finish of the Tomek House, there is Robie's corduroy brickwork. And instead of the simple wooden gutters of the Tomek roof, the Robie gutters are broad sheaths of copper upturned in a way that makes one think of the planing edge of a bird's wing (figs. 42 and 43). Indeed, they make the roof appear to glide and hover. The Tomek House has no balcony, and without it as a foil, the cantilever seems ever so slightly less daring. It is the balcony that allowed Wright to turn a whole wall of the Robie living and dining rooms to glass doors and windows without sacrifice of privacy. The Tomek living and dining rooms are partly connected by the flow of space along the windows, but in the Robie House the two rooms are fused still further, even to the point of cutting an aperture through the chimney. Entrance to the Tomek House is simple and direct, while that to the Robie House is circuitous and oblique. One searches hard for the Robie door, and one's first impression is that a gangplank is needed to board this strange vessel of the future that somehow drifted in and ran aground in the Hyde Park of 1909.

Figure 42. Tomek House, roof gutter (Margaret Olin)   Figure 43. Robie House, roof gutter (Margaret Olin)

Figure 44. Robie House, chimney
(Margaret Olin)

But the most interesting difference between the two houses is traceable to the perspective proof. The urban grid and the narrower corner site conspired to make the diagonal view of the Robie House the dominant and privileged view. The crossing of 58th Street and Woodlawn Avenue was the vantage point chosen by most early photographers, and obviously the one favored by Wright himself. What we must imagine is a preliminary plan of the Robie House similar to the Ullman drawing, with radiant lines of sight drawn from this corner to intersect the whole design. Then we have to imagine the architect "pulling" a perspective proof and checking to see if every element was adequate to the requirements of the eye. Some things presumably failed the test, and one can find their corrections in the final building. One can imagine the bedroom roof being stretched or the boundary walls pulled further out to catch the diagonal view, but the most conspicuous revision was in the chimney. It is as though Wright felt that a flat chimney of the Tomek sort offered too slender a target to the perspective view, like a duellist who offers an unfairly narrow profile to his opponent (figs. 38, 39). So the Robie chimney was changed to an L-shaped design that catches the diagonal view more forcefully (fig. 44). In fact it is part chimney and part mirage. The narrow foot of the L is really a simple closet clad in brick (fig. 45).[68] It receives no direct support from below, and in spite of extra steel beams at this point, the living room ceiling sags noticeably under the added weight. The whole ingenious fraud is exposed by an opening that connects this closet with a small rooftop balcony. Wright no sooner establishes the illusion of mass than he deflates it with this glass door. He acknowledges the importance of perspective, but not without a wink.

What is interesting about the sequence Robie 1 to 4, and in particular about the jump from the Tomek to the Robie House, is that it allows us to see Wright standing in front of his own work and criticizing it. Very few modern visitors are tempted to be as critical as Wright himself apparently was with his own work. For most people the Tomek House would be progressive enough. It is a superb design in the abstract, but also a very appealing place to live. Behind the broadside facade, with all its daring new ideas, stands a large, generous block of a house, and on the inside, intimacy is never sacrificed for grandeur of effect. It strikes a classic balance that one would hardly want to alter. Only Wright would have been capable of the imaginative dissatisfaction that led to the Robie House. He pushed every idea to the limit allowed by a much more generous budget. Paradoxically, the richer man ended up in the more radical house. There is something of the quality of a demonstration piece in the Robie House, of ideas taken to an extreme, that explains why so few visitors feel they would want to live there. Wright later called it ''a good house for a good man,''[69] but it transcends the personality of Robie or any single owner and emerges as a great and enduring work of art, one that had to be designed four times before reaching maturity.

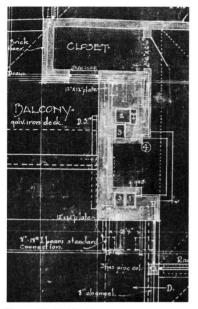

Figure 45. Robie House, blueprint detail showing chimney, closet and balcony (University of Chicago Archives, Joseph Regenstein Library, © 1984 by The Frank Lloyd Wright Foundation)

Figure 46. Taliesin, Wisconsin, detail of roofs (Wendingen 1925)

□ □ □ □ CONCLUSION □ □ □ □

The Robie House contributed to a totally new conception of the facade and thus broke with an age-old tradition in architecture. For centuries the facade had been the static face of a building, solid, symmetrical, and set at right angles to the axis of approach. Wright's early houses fall squarely in this tradition, particularly the Charnley, Blossom, and Winslow Houses of 1891–93. The Heller House of 1897 gives the first hint of something new, with two facades set at the ends of an L-shaped plan meant to be seen in perspective.[70] Perspective grows in importance, thanks presumably to Wright's own response to the photographs and renderings in which he presented his houses and to the device of the perspective proof. Gradually the interlocking masses of the prairie house grow more complex until the facade in the conventional sense disappears. What takes its place is something more dynamic, an interwoven image, a crossing of trajectories made by balconies and roofs that appear to have hurtled past each other on a near collision course.

In October 1909, seven months after work on the Robie House had begun, Wright turned the final stages of construction over to assistants and permanently abandoned his Oak Park practice.[71] He left his home and family in order to travel to Europe and consummate a love affair with the wife of a former client, Mrs. Mamah Borthwick Cheney, whose house he had designed in 1904. The affair was the catalyst for a break that had many roots in his personal and professional life. He had grown estranged from his wife and their six children. He had achieved enormous professional success, but still felt that he had not received his due of "honest genuine criticism," as he complained to the critic Harriet Monroe in 1907.[72] He had lost a commission that might have secured for his architecture the ultimate stamp of social approval, the McCormick mansion in Lake Forest, for which he had prepared designs in 1907 but which went instead to the Renaissance-revival architect Charles A. Platt. He felt stifled by the suburban mores of Oak Park and had already been told (by the visiting philosopher Kuno Francke, for one) that true recognition of his achievement would only come in Europe. His official destination was Berlin, home of the architectural publisher Wasmuth, who had invited Wright to prepare a monograph on his work. After a visit to Berlin, he spent the year between October 1909 and October 1910 working on this enterprise in Florence and Fiesole. After this, he returned to his Oak Park home for less than a year, and in August 1911 he moved to Wisconsin, where he had started a new home, Taliesin, for Mamah Cheney, and where the two lived together until Mamah's tragic murder in August 1914.

Since the break of 1909 seems so complete, and since it was followed by still further breaks after Wright's move to Tokyo and California after 1916, one might ask how much of what he learned on the Robie House survived and left its mark on his later work. There are many projects of this period in which the importance formerly attached to perspective begins to decline. In the design for the Banff National Park Pavilion in Canada of 1911–12,[73] for example, Wright returned to the broadside view and the axial symmetry of the Yahara Boat Club and the River Forest Tennis Club. The plans of Midway Gardens in Chicago and the Imperial Hotel in Tokyo are as symmetrical as the most formal products of the École des Beaux-Arts.[74] However, there are details here and there that recall the idea of crossing trajectories, like a pair of small roofs in Taliesin (fig. 46). And what a recent study has called "diagonal planning" continues to develop in unexecuted projects of the 1920s.[75] In Europe this aspect of Wright's work began to bear fruit. A plan and photograph of the Robie House were illustrated in an article by the Dutch architect J. J. P. Oud in *De Stijl* in 1918, and a year later Robt. Van'T Hoff quoted the passage from Wright's 1908 essay "In the Cause of Architecture" that concludes, "A perspective may be a proof but it is no nurture."[76] Their own Wrightian houses are relatively blocky and symmetrical, but they helped to transmit the idea of perspective proof to an important early project by Mies van der Rohe, his brick country house of 1923 (fig. 47). Important aspects of Mies's plan, particularly the way space flows freely around walls that hardly ever touch, were inspired by De Stijl paintings, in particular the compositions of Theo Van Doesburg.[77] But unlike these models, the whole design is engineered to come off best in the perspective view. Mies had understood the Robie design.

By 1935 Wright himself had returned to many of these principles in the design of Fallingwater, Edgar Kaufmann's famous house over a waterfall in the stream called Bear Run in Ohiopyle, Pennsylvania. As Donald Hoffmann has shown, Fallingwater was laid out by setting one side of a 30–60° triangle along the line of the falls and then aligning the structure with the other sides.[78] Thus if the house was photogenic it was not by accident. The picturesque view from a boulder downstream, enshrined in the famous Hedrich-Blessing photograph (fig. 48), was built into the design from the start, and to make sure the visitor took it in, a set of stairs was cut into the riverbank leading down to the chosen viewpoint. What the Chicago grid did automatically for the Robie House had to be imposed artificially on the Pennsylvania wilderness. Changes were introduced into the initial plan that show the effects of the perspective proof. The kitchen area, which began as a glass box at the extreme left end of the design, was changed into an L-shaped mass of stone and made into a more central fulcrum. The tall glass window that runs up through the middle of this mass to a height of three stories is a descendant of the tiny glass door in the Robie chimney. Two terraces (one short and one very long) were added to the stone fulcrum on the left, and new trellises were added to the great balconies on the right. Together these details create the feeling of aerodynamic flow. From the classic downstream view Fallingwater seems to be made up of the trajectories of terraces that have nearly collided in flight.

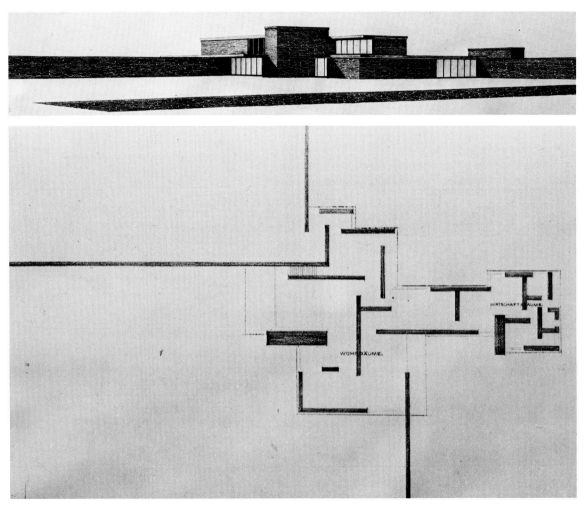

Figure 47. Ludwig Mies van der Rohe, project for a brick country house, 1923
(Mies van der Rohe Archive, The Museum of Modern Art, New York, Gift of Ludwig Mies van der Rohe)

The reason why Wright returned with such intense conviction in 1935 to ideas developed in the Robie House has to do with the way he saw himself and his career at the moment Fallingwater was conceived.[79] For several years he had gone without commissions. The grandiose projects of the late 1920s had all remained on paper. Nearing 70, he was left to write and reminisce, exhibit and lecture, teach the Taliesin apprentices and envision an ideal America in the projects for Broadacre City. But his active career was generally considered over. Furthermore, a new historiography of modern architecture had sprung up in which Wright was assigned to a kind of transitional, grandfather generation, called the "New Tradition" in Hitchcock's epoch-making book of 1929.[80] Along with designers of the Arts and Crafts movement and of Art Nouveau, he had pointed the way to a promised land that he would never himself enter. He was considered a romantic individualist in perpetual revolt against the shackles of a fixed style. In 1932 Hitchcock and Johnson gave him credit for embracing the machine and for inventing open planning: "Wagner, Behrens and Perret lightened the solid massiveness of traditional architecture; Wright dynamited it."[81] But he was not included with the younger generation that Hitchcock called the "New Pioneers," who were charting the course of the modern movement.

Naturally, Wright had his own view of the New Pioneers. They were for him like former comrades gone astray, the unfunctional "functionalist" wing of what had once been a common cause. Far from merely dismissing them, he took up an active polemic against them in his writings of the early 1930s. They were *simplistes,* taking ideas Wright felt he had invented and sterilizing them into hardened and heartless reductions of the originals. They only grasped one quarter of the matter (the new simplicity brought about by the machine), omitting the other three quarters, which had to do with the nature of materials, integral ornament, and the third dimension. To prove that he had celebrated the machine earlier than anybody else, he opened his Princeton lectures of 1931 by reading his own early lecture "The Art and Craft of the Machine," first delivered in 1901.[82] But he denied that the house is literally a machine (meaning Corbusier's "machine for living in"), "except in the same sense that our hearts are suction pumps." He maintained that he had tried to reintroduce the quality of ro-

Figure 48. Kaufmann House, Fallingwater, 1935–36 (Bill Hedrich, Hedrich-Blessing)

mance into architecture, "this quality of the *heart*, the essential joy we have in living." "Our architecture itself would become a poor, flat-faced thing of steel-bones, box-outlines, gas-pipe and hand-rail fittings . . . without this essential *heart* beating in it." Romance becomes associated with the third dimension, and its antithesis became what he called the cardboard house.[83]

Wright knew the International Style only through photographs,[84] and many of its subtleties eluded him. For instance, it might be said that Corbusier's ideal in the Villa Stein at Garches of 1927 was to pack a set of terraces into a box. The early drawings show how rambling these terraces were and how much discipline was needed to compress them into a very dense and thoughtful cube.[85] But to Wright the photographs showed just another cardboard box. He had certainly done better before and could do better still. Idled, pushed from the limelight by a new generation of radicals, itching to reappropriate forms that he felt had been plundered from his own early work, conscious of his reputation as a dynamiter of boxes, Wright seized his chance with Fallingwater. He took concrete terraces and exploded them outward from a central core. Older ideas like the perspective view, the cantilevers, and the image of crossing trajectories took on a new importance because they were ways of reintroducing the third dimension, and with it a symbolism of romance. Fallingwater was a very daring building in a structural sense, but also in the slightly shocking way that elements from different visual worlds were combined. The terraces and concrete slabs were retrieved from Europe, whither they had strayed from Wright's own work. But no European modernist would have combined them with the rustic stonework that goes back through Taliesin and Wright's early work to Richardson's use of boulders and to a view of the natural house originating in Olmsted and Emerson.[86] And the principles according to which these elements are combined, the perspective proof and the images of frozen movement, go back to the world of the Robie House. Even if much had been jettisoned from the Oak Park years by 1935, these principles survived in a building that is one of the great critiques of the modern movement in architecture, and simultaneously one of its masterpieces.

LETTER FROM FRANK LLOYD WRIGHT TO HARRIET MONROE

Harriet Monroe (1860–1936) was a Chicago poet and critic who is also known for her biography of the architect John Wellborn Root, her brother-in-law. On 13 April 1907 she wrote a review in the *Chicago Examiner* of the exhibition sponsored by the Architectural Club at the Art Institute of Chicago. Wright's work featured prominently in the exhibition and in the review. She was sympathetic to Wright's house designs but reserved about his monumental buildings. She criticized the "plaster models for Unity Church at Oak Park, for the Larkin Company administration building at Buffalo, and for a huge, square nameless structure, all of which look too much like fantastic blockhouses, full of corners and angles and squat, square columns, massive and weighty, without grace or ease or monumental beauty." Wright was furious and wrote her the letter reproduced below. Reading it, one catches a glimpse of him pounding out his ideas on the typewriter (the same one used to draft the specifications for the Robie House), fum-

bling for words and careless of syntax but on fire with a vision of a new American architecture. It is a forceful statement of the ideals behind the prairie house, and parts were later incorporated into his essay of 1908, "In the Cause of Architecture" (*Architectural Record* 23 [March 1908]: 155–221). Later Wright felt he had been slightly harsh with Harriet Monroe and soon sent her a note to that effect, a portion of which is reproduced below following the original letter. They remained in touch. She visited him in Taliesin, reviewed his work again in 1914, and was invited by him to write an article on his work for the *New York Record*.

Four letters from Wright, including the two reproduced here, are preserved in the Harriet Monroe Poetry Collection in the Department of Special Collections of the Joseph Regenstein Library at the University of Chicago. Robert C. Twombly called attention to them in *Frank Lloyd Wright: An Interpretive Biography* (New York: Harper and Row, 1973), pp. 94–96. Monroe's review has been published (but without Wright's reply) in H. Allen Brooks, ed., *Writings on Wright* (Cambridge, Mass.: M.I.T. Press, 1981), pp. 111–13. Reyner Banham discusses

Monroe as a critic in his introduction to the reprint of Harriet Monroe, *John Wellborn Root: A Study of His Life and Work* (1896; facsimile, Park Forest, Ill.: Prairie School Press, 1966).

Postmarked April 18, 1907

My dear Miss Monroe—and at the beginning let me say that to me "My dear Miss Monroe" for the moment is a TYPE and this rude but not ill-natured resentment is inscribed to the "type."

Architects have learned, long since, that the professional critic's commodity, when related to architecture at least either has to be "steered" from the inside or intelligently so prejudiced or deliberately manufactured so or it is quite apt to be of the "I-may-not-know-what-Art-is-but-I-know-what-I-like" variety,—bromidic and utterly useless.

Personally, I am hungry for the honest, genuine criticism that searches the soul of the thing and sifts its form. Praise isn't needed especially. There is enough of that, such as it is, but we all need intelligent painstaking inquiry leading into the nature of the proposition to be characterized before with airy grace the subject is lightly touched up with House Beautiful English for the mob.

The struggle behind vital work of any kind is naturally difficult enough but it is precisely the Harriet Monroe in this sense in society that makes the struggle unnecessarily grim and temporarily thankless. Her commodity has no power to harm the inherent virtue of good work but it does serve to hamper the man and to confuse and hinder a practical issue that deserves all the help and strength that, grudgingly enough in any case, may come to it from a public in these matters diffident or indifferent. Fashion and Sham rule the day. When an independent effort to be true to a worthy ideal has the courage to lift its head it deserves something more than the capricious slap-stick of "the type," even if the slap appeals to the gallery, in other words to "our very best people."

Personally, again, I have met little more than the superficial snap-judgement insult of the "artistically informed." I am quite used to it, glad to owe it nothing in any final outcome. But, meanwhile the *Cause* suffers delay! That is the price the public pays for "the type" and it is the serious side of the matter.

I cannot believe you altogether insensible to fundamental qualities but what a flimsy characterization of the Ideal behind the work to which I have given my life, you have on record!—"The old orders all worked out," (starting to do a new stunt to bring down "the gallery" too, I suppose). "Progress before precedent" perhaps? Believe me, dear Miss Monroe, it is all not one half so silly. Need I say that it is the very spirit that gave life to the old forms that this work courts? That it is the true inspiration that made of the time honored precedent in its own time a living thing that it craves? Venerable traditional forms are held by this work still too sacred to be paraded as a meretricious mask for the indecencies and iniquities of the marketplace!

Long ago, yes ages ago, from Nature came inspiration to the Architect and back to Nature with the principles deduced from these dead forms or formulae we will go again for inspiration. I know we shall find it for the Gods still live.

In the average of this work you saw merely a curious experiment with certain boxes, withal a "square" and a "squat" that offended your dainty love of fleshly curves and sensuous graces, a love that after all is in the last analysis rather cheap and not merely because it is common. But, is it impossible that the exquisite delicacy of the living nature that we all love may bloom more vividly where the "Architectural," which is primarily the background for this life, itself becomes a more quiet and restrained convention than has yet been practiced? Why usurp what by nature belongs to the other members of the family—Sculpture, Painting, Literature and Music? For one I decline to be obsessed as are most artists and almost all arts by the Literal or by Literature. My conception of the architectural art is somewhat higher than that.

Need I remind you that the pyramid is just a pyramid—that's all—the obelisk a huge billet of stone upended?—a Greek temple a rectangle with angular excrescences?—the Farnesi a box with a lid?

Perhaps it might be well to mention in this connection that one of the "huge," formless, nameless structures of your story was a small scale plaster model for a cast concrete column for Unity Church. In the edifice the column itself stands two feet six inches by thirteen feet high. This is one of the buildings wherein imagination halts!

Concerning our perennial friend, the "squat"—we happen to be living on the prairie. The prairie has a beauty of its own. A building on the prairie should recognize the features of its quiet level and accentuate them harmoniously. It should be quiet, broad, inclusive, a welcome associate of trees and flowers not a nervous, fussy interloper, and should be "married" to the ground. Hence, broad, sheltering eaves over determined masses, gentle roofs, spreading base and outreaching walls.

What is publicly set forth in this little collection could hardly be American Architecture. No—not yet—but I say that if a given type, (like the type or like it not) be handled with the *organic consistency* and such individuality as is manifest in this aggregation here, then, an American Architecture is a possibility and will be a definite probability when conscientious efforts of this nature wherever they may be found, receive the encouragement on their native heath that they already have received in conservative Old England or in France where these square, squat experiments with boxes have been accorded the rare virtue of originality without eccentricity. Buildings, like people, must be honest, must be sincere and withal as lovable and gracious as may be. But, unfortunately for the man who dares, we as a people, artistically, have a deadly and painfully provincial horror of doing the "incorrect thing" which the self-conscious dangerous small-knowledge of the provincial

art critic only serves to intensify, making it just so much more difficult for us as a people to come into our own.

Someday, as Mc Andrews prayed in his "Hymn," even the "first class passenger" will understand that the classic is no matter of the dead letter of former glory and will know that the old spirit which was so vital then is vital now and living in forms the newspapers pronounce eccentric. They may even proclaim that after all these forms are truly classic in the best sense of that much abused term.

But why be serious? Are not the limitations already obvious and fixed? The progress made already marked in the public prints by such shoddy fustian from the architectural rag-bag, as "Ottenheimer's clock," such cheneille as "Wilson's graceful residences"?

Sincerely,
Frank Lloyd Wright

From an undated letter to Harriet Monroe

Robbed by the innate modesty of a difficult nature I am denied the consolation offered: but, to My dear Miss Monroe I apologize for the serious moment in her behalf. It was occasioned by my first sight of her a week ago last Friday afternoon, when I conceived that the type was unworthy of her.

Anyhow, Whistler had his "Arry,"—now have I not my "Arriet"?

Hers and henceforth hers only,
Frank Lloyd Wright

NOTES

□   □   □   □

1. G. W. Sheldon, *Artistic Country-Seats: Types of Recent American Villa and Cottage Architecture with Instances of Country Club-Houses* (New York: D. Appleton, 1886), 1:46; Vincent Scully, *The Shingle Style and the Stick Style* (New Haven: Yale University Press, 1971), pp. 120–21 and figs. 93–94.

2. "Mr. Robie Knew What He Wanted," *Architectural Forum* 109 (October 1958): 126–27, 206, and 210, reprinted in Leonard K. Eaton, *Two Chicago Architects and Their Clients: Frank Lloyd Wright and Howard Van Doren Shaw* (Cambridge, Mass.: M.I.T. Press, 1969), pp. 126–33. This interview has been supplemented recently by an interview with Robie's daughter, Irma Strauss, "An Interview with Lorraine Robie O'Connor," *Frank Lloyd Wright Newsletter* 3, no. 4 (1980): 1–3.

3. John Lloyd Wright, *My Father Who Is On Earth* (New York: G. P. Putnam's Sons, 1946), p. 148.

4. Floyd Clymer, *Treasury of Early American Automobiles, 1877–1925* (New York: Bonanza, 1950), p. 209.

5. The car wash is mentioned in the specifications, and the pit is shown on the ground floor plan of the blueprints, in the left hand garage. For these documents, see the Bibliography.

6. John Lloyd Wright, *My Father*, p. 50.

7. John B. Rae, *American Automobile Manufacturers: The First Forty Years* (Philadelphia, 1959), especially pp. 8–15, 25, 72, 105–9; Daniel J. Boorstin, *The Americans: The Democratic Experience* (New York: Random, 1974), pp. 57–62; and William Greenleaf, *Monopoly on Wheels: Henry Ford and The Selden Automobile Patent* (Detroit: Wayne State University Press, 1961).

8. "Mr. Robie Knew What He Wanted," in Eaton, *Two Chicago Architects*, p. 128. Eaton's fundamental study of Wright's patronage is the source for the remarks that follow.

9. Frank Lloyd Wright, "In the Cause of Architecture," *Architectural Record* 23 (March 1908): 158; the quotation is taken from the reprint in *Wendingen*, 1965 facsimile, p. 12.

10. "Mr. Robie Knew What He Wanted," in Eaton, *Two Chicago Architects*, p. 128.

11. Alfred H. Granger, "An Architect's Studio," *House Beautiful,* December 1899, pp. 36–45 (with the earliest photographs of the interior); Robert C. Spencer, Jr., "The Work of Frank Lloyd Wright," *Architectural Review* (Boston), vol. 7, June 1900, fold-out plate of the studio with information on the plans for a circulating library (reprinted as Robert C. Spencer, Jr., *The Work of Frank Lloyd Wright from 1893 to 1900* [Park Forest, Ill.: Prairie School Press, 1964]). The library is fully documented in the pamphlet by Donald Kalec and Thomas Heinz, *Frank Lloyd Wright Home and Studio, Oak Park, Illinois* (Oak Park: Frank Lloyd Wright Home and Studio Foundation, 1975); and in the larger compendium by the Frank Lloyd Wright Home and Studio Foundation, *The Plan for Restoration and Adaptive Use of the Frank Lloyd Wright Home and Studio* (Chicago: University of Chicago Press, 1978).

12. Frank Lloyd Wright, *Ausgeführte Bauten und Entwürfe,* 2 vols. (Berlin: Ernst Wasmuth, 1910) (abbreviated here as Wasmuth 1910). The smaller volume of photographs produced the following year is *Frank Lloyd Wright Ausgeführte Bauten* (Berlin: Ernst Wasmuth, 1911) (abbreviated here as Wasmuth 1911), reproduced in facsimile as *Frank Lloyd Wright: The Early Work,* with an Introduction by Edgar Kaufmann, Jr. (New York: Horizon, 1968). All references are to the facsimile.

Wright talks about the 1910 portfolio in a letter of that year to C. R. Ashbee: "The monograph [i.e., Wasmuth 1910] giving the office ideal,—the architects rendering of his vision—his scheme graphically proposed in his own manner—the Sonderheft [i.e., Wasmuth 1911], the photographs, of the results in brick and mortar." (Alan Crawford, "Ten Letters from Frank Lloyd Wright to Charles Robert Ashbee," *Architectural History* 13 (1970): 68).

13. "Mr. Robie Knew What He Wanted," in Eaton, *Two Chicago Architects,* p. 127. On p. 130 Robie has Wright say that he was about to leave Oak Park in 1909 for Japan to build an earthquake-proof hotel. Of course, Wright was leaving for Germany not Japan, and Robie's confusion apparently resulted from his recollection of the account of the Imperial Hotel in *An Autobiography* (London: Longmans, Green, 1932), pp. 221–23; 2d ed., New York: Duell, Sloan and Pearce, 1943, pp. 222–23.

14. "Mr. Robie Knew What He Wanted," in Eaton, *Two Chicago Architects,* p. 127.

15. Wasmuth 1910, unpaginated preface.

16. Frank Lloyd Wright, "In the Cause," in *Wendingen,* 1965 facsimile, p. 21.

17. Spencer, "The Work of Frank Lloyd Wright," 1964 reprint, p. 62. Spencer is quoting a passage of Louis Sullivan and applying it to Wright.

18. See section 6 of the Bibliography.

19. The child is the same as the boy identified as Fred Robie, Jr., by his sister, Lorraine Robie O'Connor, in Strauss, "An Interview," p. 2.

20. Strauss, "An Interview," p. 1.

21. Jordy relates this aspect of Wright to Sullivan's mode of design, "an interlocked composition of components initially shaped by the simplest geometry" (William Jordy, *Progressive and Academic Ideals at the Turn of the Twentieth Century* [New York: Doubleday, 1972], p. 199).

22. For the dates see Grant Manson, *Frank Lloyd Wright to 1910: The First Golden Age* (New York: Reinhold, 1958), p. 216.

23. According to information from the University of Chicago Development Office, the long Roman bricks made available when the driveway wall was lowered to its present height were used to construct a small annex immediately to the east of the garage. The annex was demolished in 1976, but many of the bricks were preserved and are in storage underneath the front porch.

24. Henry-Russell Hitchcock, "Frank Lloyd Wright and the 'Academic Tradition' of the Early Eighteen-Nineties," *Journal of the Warburg and Courtauld Institutes* 7 (1944): 46–63. See the equally classic treatment of Wright's sources in Scully, *The Shingle Style,* pp. 113–64.

25. Hitchcock, " 'Academic Tradition,' " pl. 14a–b, and Scully, *The Shingle Style,* figs. 149, 150, for photographs of the Taylor House. The Blossom House is illustrated in Jordy, *Progressive and Academic Ideals,* p. 186, figs. 77, 78; Henry-Russell Hitchcock, *In the Nature of Materials:*

The Buildings of Frank Lloyd Wright, 1887–1941 (New York: Duell, 1942, reprinted New York: Da Capo, 1973, figs. 19, 20; and Manson, Frank Lloyd Wright to 1910, p. 49.

Four plans and four elevations showing the Blossom House in its original condition are preserved in the form of black line prints in the Burnham Library of the Art Institute of Chicago (Special 724.91 W94 cl). They were made from original drawings in the possession of Mrs. Charles F. Haseltine, owner of the house in 1940.

26. My source for these concepts and quotations is the Froebel textbook by Maria Kraus-Boelte and John Kraus, The Kindergarten Guide (New York, 1881), vol. 1, especially pp. 32–38 and 176.

The early sources for the influence of Froebel on Wright are Spencer, "The Work of Frank Lloyd Wright," (1900), 1964 reprint p. 69 (where continuity is stressed between Wright's early Froebel training and his apprenticeship under Sullivan); and Wright, Autobiography, 1932 ed., p. 11, 1943 ed., pp. 13–14. Recent treatments include Grant Manson, "Wright in the Nursery," Architectural Review (London) 113 (June 1953): 349–51; Manson, Frank Lloyd Wright to 1910, pp. 5–10; Richard MacCormac, "The Anatomy of Wright's Aesthetic," Architectural Review (London) 143 (February 1968): 143–46, with somewhat excessive emphasis on Wright's use of a grid to produce his plans; Edgar Kaufmann, Jr., "'Form Became Feeling': A New View of Froebel and Wright," Journal of the Society of Architectural Historians 40 (1981): 130–37, with the hypothesis that Wright's mother may have encountered Froebel's system during her youth in Wisconsin, and with considerable deemphasis of Froebel's contribution to Wright's sense of interior space. There are further observations by the same author, with new material from the Taliesin archives, in "Frank Lloyd Wright's Mementos of Childhood," Journal of the Society of Architectural Historians 41 (1982): 232–37.

27. Wright, Autobiography, 1932 ed., p. 11, 1943 ed., pp. 13–14.

28. This interesting approach, which makes Froebel a conscious rediscovery on the part of the mature Wright, is taken by Vincent Scully in his Foreword to

David Hanks, The Decorative Designs of Frank Lloyd Wright (New York: E. P. Dutton, 1979), p. xiv.

29. Compare the plan of the windmill, a diamond wedged into a polygon, with the Froebel stick pattern illustrated in Kraus-Boelte and Kraus, Kindergarten Guide, p. 251. The windmill is illustrated in Manson, Frank Lloyd Wright to 1910, p. 93, fig. 71, but its correct date is the one documented in Robert Twombly, Frank Lloyd Wright: An Interpretive Biography (New York: Harper and Row, 1973), p. 49 n. (September 1897).

30. Louis Sullivan, "Emotional Architecture as Compared with Classical," Inland Architect and News Record 24, no. 4 (November 1894): 32–34.

31. Two of the three windows on the north side of the house are now blocked, but they were originally open, as shown on all early plans. The original height of the driveway wall in front of the garage was exactly level with the sill of these three windows. From the street the spectator could look over the wall, through the post-and-lintel grid, through the windows on the south side of the kitchen, and out the windows on the north side.

32. According to Robie, Wright took a special trip to St. Louis to have this brick made, each brick being 1⅝ inches thick and 11⅝ inches long ("Mr. Robie Knew What He Wanted," in Eaton, Two Chicago Architects, p. 132). In the contractor's specifications (p. 8), all exposed walls were to be faced with brick costing $35.00 per thousand (crossed out and changed to $26.00), "horizontal joints wide and white, vertical joints narrow and colored to match brick. Horizontal joints raked out as approved." Wright picked the Robie House along with the Cheney House and the Imperial Hotel as examples of his best brickwork (see Frank Lloyd Wright, "In the Cause of Architecture, V: The Meaning of Materials—The Kiln," Architectural Record 63 (June 1928): 555–61).

33. The best treatment of the neighborhood in general and of Woodlawn Avenue in particular is Jean Block, Hyde Park Houses: An Informal History, 1856–1910 (Chicago: University of Chicago Press, 1978), especially pp. 122–24, 132–33, and figs. 60, 68–76. Wright's approach to

the problem of a narrow site has been discussed briefly for two other houses: the De Rhodes House in South Bend, Indiana, of 1906 (C. E. Percival, "Making the Most of a Narrow Lot," *House Beautiful,* July 1906, pp. 20–21); and the first Jacobs House of 1936 (Herbert Jacobs, with Katherine Jacobs, *Building with Frank Lloyd Wright* [San Francisco: Chronicle Books, 1978], p. 17).

34. "Mr. Robie Knew What He Wanted," in Eaton, *Two Chicago Architects,* p. 129. See also the survey of the property mentioned in the Bibliography, where the lot is shown to include a ten foot strip taken from the neighboring lot to the north.

35. David Van Zanten, "H. H. Richardson's Glessner House, Chicago, 1886–1887," *Journal of the Society of Architectural Historians* 23 (1964): 106–11; and James O'Gorman, *H. H. Richardson and His Office* (exhibition catalog) (Cambridge, Mass., Harvard College Library, 1974), pp. 87–91, particularly the garden plan in fig. 9b on p. 89.

36. Letter of Frank Lloyd Wright to Harriet Monroe, postmarked April 18, 1907, reprinted in full in the Appendix; and Wright, "In the Cause" (1908), in *Wendingen,* 1965 facsimile, pp. 19, 22. The idea of a house designed to blossom in season has been explored in an unpublished Harvard senior paper by Daniel Bluestone, " 'Landscape Works': Olmsted and Richardson at North Easton," ca. 1977.

37. Wasmuth 1910, pl. 37.

38. Wasmuth 1911, p. 112. This photograph was taken by the Chicago Architectural Photographing Company; an unretouched version is shown in Jordy, *Progressive and Academic Ideals,* p. 198, fig. 84.

39. Manson, *Frank Lloyd Wright to 1910,* p. 67, fig. 47. The house that makes way for a tree already standing on the site is the theme of the Misses Appleton House of 1883–84 in Lenox, Mass., by McKim, Mead, and White (Sheldon, *Artistic Country-Seats,* 1:61–65; Scully, *The Shingle Style,* pp. 143–45 and figs. 142, 143). Wright knew this house through the plates in Sheldon and copied its plan in one of his earliest projects for a house, the "Drawing shown to Lieber Meister when applying for a job" of 1887 or 1888. The plan of the "Lieber Meister" project is shown under a different name in Spencer, "The Work of Frank Lloyd Wright" (1900), 1964 ed., p. 64, and in Alberto Izzo and Camillo Gubitosi, *Frank Lloyd Wright Disegni 1887–1959* (exhibition catalog) (Florence: Centro Di, 1976), cat. nos. 1, 3. The "Lieber Meister" drawing has been thought to date from a later period, ca. 1893–99 (Eileen Michels, "The Early Drawings of Frank Lloyd Wright Reconsidered," *Journal of the Society of Architectural Historians* 30 (1971): 302), but the connection with the Appleton plan makes the early date entirely convincing.

40. Spencer, "The Work of Frank Lloyd Wright" (1900), 1964 reprint, p. 66.

41. The sliding screen is shown on the blueprints, while the iron grilles appear in many photographs, especially in Hanks, *Decorative Designs,* p. 109, fig. 109.

42. The destination of the ice was the (nonelectric) refrigerator mentioned on p. 16 of the specifications.

43. The original doorframe, shown in Wasmuth 1910, pl. 37, and in an old photograph on display in the house, was reused as the inside door of the present pair.

44. Specifications, p. 20, and the unpaginated preface to Wasmuth 1910: "A type of structure especially suited to the prairie will be found in the Coonley, Thomas, Heurtley, Tomek and Robie houses, which are virtually one floor arrangements, raised a low story height above the level of the ground."

45. In his forthcoming monograph, David Hoffmann will reconstruct the original appearance of the interior and emphasize the way in which the missing screens and portieres originally gave clear definition to every room.

46. Spencer, "The Work of Frank Lloyd Wright" (1900), 1964 reprint, p. 67. On Wright and the open plan see now H. Allen Brooks, "Frank Lloyd Wright and the Destruction of the Box," *Journal of the Society of Architectural Historians* 38 (1979): 7–14.

47. The prominent role played by the hearth in Wright's symbolism of the family nucleus is traced

back to the writings of Gottfried Semper in the perceptive essay by Rosemarie Bletter, "On Martin Fröhlich's Gottfried Semper," *Oppositions.* October 1974, p. 151.

48. On pp. 18–20 of the specifications, the contractor is obliged to install a heating plant that would maintain a temperature of 70 degrees when it is 10 degrees below zero outside. Wright's technical achievement at the Robie House is studied by Reyner Banham, *The Architecture of the Well-Tempered Environment* (Chicago: University of Chicago Press, 1969), pp. 115–21.

49. Donald Kalec, "The Prairie School Furniture," *Prairie School Review* 1, no. 4 (1964): 5–21; Hanks, *Decorative Designs,* pp. 50, 105–10; and Strauss, "An Interview," p. 2. According to information kindly provided by Katherine Lee Keefe, nine dining room chairs from the Robie House are in the possession of the David and Alfred Smart Gallery of the University of Chicago; one of them has a higher seat to accommodate a child.

50. On the relationship between Wright's architecture, the ritual of dining, and Chicago social customs around 1910 see Norris Kelley Smith, *Frank Lloyd Wright: A Study in Architectural Content* (1966; reprint, Watkins Glenn, N.Y.: American Life Foundation, 1979), pp. 87–90, and the more balanced and worldly approach in Twombly, *Frank Lloyd Wright,* pp. 70–76. Wright designed furnishings not to tyrannize his clients or manipulate their lives but because he considered architecture the consummation of the arts, encompassing all the others. Interesting parallels with the self-conception of Charles Rennie Mackintosh, who also considered it his artistic responsibility to create total interior designs, are drawn by Thomas Howarth, *Charles Rennie Mackintosh and the Modern Movement* (London: Routledge, 1952), pp. 116–20, and by Roger Billcliffe, *Charles Rennie Mackintosh: The Complete Furniture, Furniture Drawings, and Interior Designs* (London: Lutterworth Press, 1979), pp. 9–10. Howarth (p. 120) recalls that "Muthesius went so far as to say that Mackintosh's rooms reached such a high level of artistic achievement that even a book bound in the wrong kind of cover might be sufficient to upset the delicate color relationships."

51. Wright, "In the Cause" (1908), in *Wendingen,* 1965 facsimile, p. 19.

52. The account book is discussed in the Bibliography. On Niedecken-Walbridge, see Hanks, *Decorative Designs,* pp. 44, 105–10, 215–17.

53. "Mr. Robie Knew What He Wanted," in Eaton, *Two Chicago Architects,* p. 131.

54. Wright, *Autobiography,* 1932 ed., p. 103, 1943, p. 106; Hitchcock, *In the Nature of Materials,* pp. 107–8, 112; and Mark Linch, "Ward Winfield Willits, a Client of Frank Lloyd Wright," *Frank Lloyd Wright Newsletter* 2, no. 2 (1979): 12.

55. Wright, *Autobiography,* 1932 ed., pp. 158–60, 1943 ed., pp. 156–58. The 1943 edition (with several variants) is the source for this and the following two quotations. Wright had already begun to articulate these ideas, in language very similar to that of his autobiography, in his article "In the Cause of Architecture, 1: The Logic of the Plan," *Architectural Record* 63 (January 1928): 49.

56. Wright, *Autobiography,* 1932 ed., p. 70, 1943 ed., pp. 70–71, a passage which is discussed in Scully, *The Shingle Style,* p. 86, n. 44.

57. Wright, *Autobiography,* 1943 ed., p. 158. The final drawing would have resembled the elevation in Izzo and Gubitosi, *Frank Lloyd Wright Disegni,* cat. no. 19. The problem confronting Wright was how to adapt a standard-sized concrete pier to both the larger temple and the smaller adjacent parish house. Classical rules of proportion, to which Wright was sensitive, demanded two sizes of pier, while the rules of economy dictated using the same wooden forms for both structures.

58. Wasmuth 1910, pl. 63.

59. Wright, "In the Cause" (1908), in *Wendingen,* 1965 facsimile, pp. 18–19.

60. Eugène Emmanuel Viollet-le-Duc, *Discourses on Architecture,* trans. Henry Van Brunt (Boston, 1875), 1:504–6, for the following quotations. Other aspects of Viollet-e-Duc's influence on Wright are presented in Donald Hoffmann, "Frank Lloyd Wright and Viollet-le-Duc,"

Journal of the Society of Architectural Historians 28 (1969): 173–83.

61. The plan is reproduced in Edgar Kaufmann, Jr., *An American Architecture: Frank Lloyd Wright* (New York: Horizon, 1955), p. 29, and in a small detail photo in MacCormac, "Anatomy of Wright's Aesthetic," p. 143. The sketch-proof is reproduced in Frank Lloyd Wright, *Drawings for a Living Architecture* (New York: Horizon, 1959), p. 222. The final, corrected plan is given in Wasmuth 1910, pl. 16. According to Hitchcock, *In the Nature of Materials,* p. 114, Wright's unexecuted project is quite different from the Ullman House actually built by Robert Spencer in 1905. There is a split-level feature in Wright's final Ullman plan—a sunken dining room—which may reflect the influence of Walter Burley Griffin, according to H. Allen Brooks, *The Prairie School: Frank Lloyd Wright and His Midwest Contemporaries* (Toronto: University of Toronto Press, 1972), pp. 80–81, n. 9.

A similar preliminary plan exists for Wright's Cheney House of 1904 (reproduced in *Drawings for a Living Architecture,* p. 156) as well as a sketch-proof in perspective (reproduced in Frank Lloyd Wright, *A Testament* [New York: Horizon, 1957], p. 52).

Sometimes Wright would have drawn the perspective proofs on the same sheet as the plans. When his son saw him at work on Midway Gardens in 1914, he observed that "an interlocking organism of plans, elevations, sections and small perspective sketches were all on the one sheet" (John Lloyd Wright, *My Father,* p. 72).

62. An example of the perspective-proof from the period just after the Robie House can be found in the form of two drawings for the San Francisco Press skyscraper of 1912. They have been published separately but not linked to this aspect of the design process. The first drawing is a proof "pulled" after the design had already progressed rather far (Izzo and Gubitosi, *Frank Lloyd Wright Disegni,* cat. no. 31). When Wright saw it he decided on some major revisions. He changed the relationship of the two towers, moved the entrance, and increased the drama of the projecting slabs. All these changes are recorded in the second drawing,

the final rendering designed to sell the idea (Arthur Drexler, *The Drawings of Frank Lloyd Wright* (New York: Horizon, 1962), cat. no. 45). It is possible that both these drawings were done by assistants, and that Wright's role in the perspective-proof was that of critic and final arbiter of the design.

63. See the Bibliography. The black-and-white perspective rendering reproduced in Drexler, *The Drawings,* cat. no. 29, is dated 1906 but certainly was drawn after the completion of the building (it shows the two hatches opened up at the last minute in the balcony). H. Allen Brooks has suggested that this whole set of expressionistic drawings, including perspectives of the Larkin Building and Unity Temple, were done much later, after Wright came to know the work of Eric Mendelsohn ("Frank Lloyd Wright and the Wasmuth Drawings," *Art Bulletin* 47 (1966): 197, n. 20). Donald Hoffmann will present evidence in his forthcoming monograph that they were actually done by an assistant to show how Wright had anticipated features of the International Style. For the first publication of the "abstract" perspective of the Robie House, see n. 83 below.

64. Wright, "In the Cause" (1908), in *Wendingen,* 1965 facsimile, p. 22.

65. Wasmuth 1910, pl. 55; Drexler, *The Drawings,* cat. nos. 6, 7; Hitchcock, *In the Nature of Materials,* p. 49 and fig. 79.

66. Wasmuth 1910, pl. 42; Wasmuth 1911, p. 97; Hitchcock, *In the Nature of Materials,* p. 115.

67. Wasmuth 1910, pl. 35; Wasmuth 1911, pp. 70–71, with the astute remarks on the house by Edgar Kaufmann on p. xvi of the 1968 facsimile; and Maya Moran, "Through a Wright Window," *Frank Lloyd Wright Newsletter* 3, no. 3 (1980): 1–4 (a sensitive analysis by an owner).

68. Banham, *Well-Tempered Environment,* p. 120, interprets the projecting limb of the chimney as a ventilating device, citing as evidence the three sets of openings in the brickwork above the glass door. It is possible that these openings do serve some minor ventilating

function, but if this part of the chimney were a major air shaft, the blueprints would certainly show it. Instead it is clearly marked as a closet, and there are no built-in flues. My argument is that design preceded function. Wright wanted the L-shaped chimney there to catch the diagonal lines of sight. Once designed, it is given a number of functions, like closet and passage to the balcony. It is also the space that gives access to the owner's safe, which is built into the main body of the brick chimney, where it would obviously stand the best chance of surviving a disastrous fire.

The L-shaped chimney with a glass door appears in embryonic form in the Heath House of 1905 in Buffalo (Wasmuth 1911, pp. 78–80).

69. "Mr. Robie Knew What He Wanted," in Eaton, *Two Chicago Architects,* p. 133.

70. Wasmuth 1911, pp. 16–17. Interesting early drawings have been published showing the Heller House at a stage closer to the Winslow stables: Spencer, "The Work of Frank Lloyd Wright" (1900), 1964 reprint, p. 63; and a similar side elevation in Frank Lloyd Wright, *Drawings for a Living Architecture,* p. 246.

71. In particular see Twombly, *Frank Lloyd Wright,* pp. 90–111, and also Manson, *Frank Lloyd Wright to 1910,* pp. 201–2, 211–13.

72. See the letter in the Appendix.

73. Drexler, *The Drawings,* cat. no. 42; William Allin Storrer, *The Architecture of Frank Lloyd Wright: A Complete Catalogue* (Cambridge, Mass.: M.I.T. Press, 1974); 2d rev. ed. 1978, no. 170, with the information that the pavilion was demolished in 1939.

74. Illustrated in *Wendingen,* 1965 facsimile, pp. 63, 108–12.

75. Neil Levine, "Frank Lloyd Wright's Diagonal Planning," in Helen Searing, ed., *In Search of Modern Architecture: A Tribute to Henry-Russell Hitchcock* (Cambridge, Mass.: M.I.T. Press, 1982), pp. 245–77. Levine traces the concept of diagonal planning from Wright's early interior spaces to the projects of the 20s and 30s, where prowlike terraces and shifts in axis are used to unite architecture and landscape.

76. J. J. P. Oud, "Architectonische Beschouwing bij Bijlage VII," *De Stijl* 1, no. 4 (February 1918): 39–41; Robt. Van'T Hoff, "Architectuur en Haar Ontwikkeling," *De Stijl* 2, no. 4 (February 1919): 40–42. Helen Searing kindly provided these references. An account of Wright's impact on Holland is presented in Reyner Banham, *Theory and Design in the First Machine Age* (London: Architectural Press, 1960), pp. 138–47.

77. Vincent Scully, "Wright vs. the International Style," *Art News,* March 1954, pp. 32–35, 64–66; and William Jordy, *The Impact of European Modernism in the Mid-Twentieth Century,* American Buildings and Their Architects, ed. W. Pierson, vol. 4 (New York: Doubleday, 1976), p. 148, figs. 63, 64. Scully (pp. 33–34) quotes an interview of 1940 in which Mies emphasized the importance of Wright's Wasmuth drawings on his whole generation, and Jordy (p. 223) quotes Mies' remark, "Before I came to Chicago I also knew about Frank Lloyd Wright and particularly about the Robie House."

78. Donald Hoffmann, *Frank Lloyd Wright's Fallingwater: The House and Its History* (New York: Dover, 1978), p. 18, where the orientation is interpreted as a means of maximizing exposure to southern sunlight. Steps to the falls are shown on the plan first published in *Architectural Forum* 68 (January 1938): 45. The diagonal view of Fallingwater is now also emphasized in Levine, "Wright's Diagonal Planning," pp. 267–68, with different nuances of interpretation.

79. The interpretation that follows was suggested in my review of Hoffmann's *Fallingwater* in the *Journal of the Society of Architectural Historians* 38 (1979): 397–98. The "double relationship" between Wright and the International Style—with Wright influencing Europe around 1910 but then showing influences from European modernism in his own work around the time of Fallingwater—is the theme of Scully, "Wright vs. the International Style," which provoked criticisms and then a reply from Scully in *Art News,* September 1954, pp. 48–49. Scully's point is important, as is his description of Fallingwater as a "creative assimilation of a host of influences—some of them originally made possible by

[Wright] himself." However, the idea of assimilation must be combined with the spirit of active attack that pervades Wright's writings of the period, and with the totally different feeling for space that Kaufmann rightly emphasizes for Fallingwater (*Art News,* September 1954, pp. 48–49). Possibly some phrase like a "polemic reexpropriation" of forms he felt he had invented could characterize Wright's stance.

80. Henry-Russell Hitchcock, *Modern Architecture: Romanticism and Reintegration* (New York: Payson and Clarke, 1929), especially pp. 115, 160, 212.

81. Henry-Russell Hitchcock and Philip Johnson, *The International Style: Architecture since 1922* (1932; reprint, New York: Norton, 1966), p. 26.

82. Frank Lloyd Wright, *Modern Architecture, Being the Kahn Lectures for 1930* (Princeton: Princeton University Press, 1931), pp. 7–23, with the quotations that follow being taken from pp. 27, 36, 39, 66–67. The Princeton lectures were reprinted in Frank Lloyd Wright, *The Future of Architecture* (New York: Horizon Press, 1953), pp. 67–182; see especially pp. 103, 106–7, 145. Wright had already reminded European readers of his "Machine" lecture in 1925 ("In the Cause of Architecture: The Third Dimension," in *Wendingen,* 1965 facsimile, p. 48). The polemic against modern architecture, particularly in its French version, is continued in Frank Lloyd Wright, *Two Lectures on Architecture* (Chicago: Art Institute, n.d. [1931]), pp. 50–53, and in the pages of the journal *T-Square* (later renamed *Shelter*) in 1932. See Norman N. Rice, "I Believe . . . ," *T-Square* 2 (January 1932): 24–25, 34–35 (promodernist); Frank Lloyd Wright, "For All May Raise the Flowers Now, For All Have Got the Seed," *T-Square* 2 (February 1932): 6–8 (polemic against the new "internationalist" eclecticism); George Howe, "Moses Turns Pharoh," *T-Square* 2 (February 1932): 9; and Frank Lloyd Wright, "Of Thee I Sing," *Shelter* 2 (April 1932): 10–12. Howe anticipates Scully's position when he says, "Why should he [Wright] who has led us out of bondage turn and destroy his children."

83. Wright, *Modern Architecture,* pp. 65–80, "The Cardboard House." In the original edition of the Princeton lectures, this chapter is introduced with a black-and-white perspective rendering of the Robie House, as though it represented the fulfillment of Wright's injunction on p. 68, "The cardboard house needs an antidote."

84. With the exception, of course, of the work of his own former disciples Rudolph Schindler and Richard Neutra in Los Angeles. In particular, Neutra's Lovell "Health" House of 1927–29 showed how features of the International Style could be adapted to American living conditions and used to dramatize a rugged, hilly site. However, a comparison of the Lovell House and Fallingwater shows how far Wright was from simply adapting features of an imported style. See Jordy, *The Impact of European Modernism,* pp. 156–57; David Gebhard, *Schindler* (New York, 1971); and Thomas S. Hines, *Richard Neutra and the Search for Modern Architecture* (New York: Oxford University Press, 1982).

85. These observations are based on the exhibition of preparatory drawings for the Villa Stein from the Foundation Le Corbusier in Paris, which was held at the Museum of Modern Art in New York in 1978. See also W. Boesiger and H. Girsberger, *Le Corbusier, 1910–65* (Zurich, 1967), pp. 54–57; and Stanislaus Von Moos, *Le Corbusier: L'architect et son mythe* (n.p., 1970), pp. 99–102).

86. The terraces of the Villa Stein and the rustic stonework of Taliesin are prophetically juxtaposed in photographs in the article by Norman Rice cited above in n. 82, which elicited a letter of response from Wright (*T-Square* 2 (February 1932): 32). Taliesin is shown in *Wendingen,* 1965 facsimile, pp. 42–51. The most rustic of Wright's early houses is the Chauncey Williams House of 1895 (Manson, *Frank Lloyd Wright to 1910,* p. 72, fig. 52), which is built on a base of boulders like Richardson's Ames Gate Lodge in North Easton, Massachusetts. The symbolism of Richardsonian stonework is explored by Bluestone in the unpublished paper mentioned above in n. 36, and in an unpublished lecture by James O'Gorman, "H. H. Richardson: The Architecture of City and Country."

▢ ▢ ▢ ▢ BIBLIOGRAPHY ▢ ▢ ▢ ▢

1. WRITINGS BY FRANK LLOYD WRIGHT TO 1938

The best way to approach Wright is through his own publications. He usually explained his work in lucid and evocative terms, and presented photographs and graphic images to complement the meaning of the text. However, it is important to keep the original chronology of the writings in mind. Wright's thought never remained static, even though he returned continually to perennial themes. Some of his early writings have been often reprinted, but with subtle changes in meaning brought about through changes in the illustrative material. The following is a list of the architect's major publications up to the time of Fallingwater, with references to recent facsimiles and to other easily accessible reprints. For a complete list, there is now an indispensable bibliography: Robert L. Sweeney, *Frank Lloyd Wright: An Annotated Bibliography* (Los Angeles: Hennessey and Ingalls, 1978).

1896–97   William C. Gannett, Frank Lloyd Wright, and William Winslow. *The House Beautiful.* River Forest, Ill.: Auvergne Press. Facsimile edition, Park Forest, Ill.: W. R. Hasbrouck, 1963. Text republished without page decorations in John Lloyd Wright, *My Father Who Is On*

Earth (New York: G. P. Putnam's Sons, 1946), pp. 153–72.

The text by the Unitarian minister William Gannett had been published in Boston in 1895; although sentimental, it did express ideas sympathetic to Wright, particularly on the ideals of domesticity and on the house not made by human hands but deposited by nature. The black-and-red page decorations were designed by Wright and printed by Winslow on a private press located in the cellar or barn of the Winslow house.

1900   Robert C. Spencer. "The Work of Frank Lloyd Wright." *Architectural Review* (Boston) 7 (June 1900): 61–72. Facsimile edition entitled *The Work of Frank Lloyd Wright from 1893 to 1900* (Park Forest, Ill.: Prairie School Press, 1964).

Spencer's text expresses many of Wright's fundamental beliefs and was obviously inspired by conversations with the architect himself. It contains a large number of invaluable photographs and drawings of Wright's early work.

1901   "The Art and Craft of the Machine." Lecture of March 1901. Reprinted in Edgar Kaufmann and Ben

Raeburn, eds., *Frank Lloyd Wright: Writings and Buildings* (New York: Horizon, 1960), pp. 55–73.

1907   Letter to Harriet Monroe, reprinted here in an Appendix.

1908   "In the Cause of Architecture." *Architectural Record* 23 (March 1908): 155–221. Text reprinted with different illustrations in the periodical *Wendingen* 7 (1925): 8–24; facsimile edition 1965. Text reprinted without illustrations in F. Gutheim, ed., *In the Cause of Architecture: Essays by Frank Lloyd Wright for Architectural Record, 1908–1952* (New York: Architectural Record, 1975), pp. 53–119.

This is the first and most important of many essays with the same title; it is the key statement of the principles informing the design of the prairie house.

1910   *Ausgeführte Bauten und Entwürfe.* 2 vols. Berlin: Ernst Wasmuth. Aside from a Japanese reprint of 1916 and a German edition of 1924, the major modern facsimiles are *Buildings, Plans, and Designs* (New York: Horizon, 1963), a large unbound portfolio; and *Ausgeführte Bauten und Entwürfe von Frank Lloyd Wright: Studies and Executed Buildings by Frank Lloyd Wright* (Palos Park, Ill.: Prairie School Press, 1975), reduced format, bound in a single volume, with both German and English texts.

The original portfolio, comprising 100 plates of plans, sections, and perspective renderings, is the major graphic source for Wright's work to 1910.

1911   *Frank Lloyd Wright: Ausgeführte Bauten.* Berlin: Ernst Wasmuth. With a Foreword by C. R. Ashbee in German, partly translated into English in an American edition. Facsimile entitled *Frank Lloyd Wright: The Early Work* (New York: Horizon and Bramhall House, 1968), with an Introduction by Edgar Kaufmann, Jr.

A smaller book by the publisher of the 1910 portfolio, consisting entirely of photographs and plans of Wright's executed buildings. The major photographic source for the period of the prairie house.

1912   *The Japanese Print: An Interpretation.* Chicago: Ralph Fletcher Seymour Company. Revised edition, New York: Horizon Press, 1967.

A major statement of Wright's aesthetic principles.

1914   "In the Cause of Architecture, Second Paper." *Architectural Record* 35 (May 1914): 405–13. Reprinted in *Wendingen*, 1965 facsimile, pp. 25–47; in Kaufmann and Raeburn, eds., *Writings and Buildings* (see 1901 above), pp. 181–96; and in F. Gutheim, ed., *In the Cause* (see 1908 above), pp. 121–29.

Contains a striking invective by Wright against many of his former associates in the Oak Park studio.

1925   *The Life-Work of the American Architect Frank Lloyd Wright.* Santpoort, Holland: C. A. Mees. A book version of seven issues of the periodical *Wendingen*, vol. 7, 1925, which were devoted to Wright. Near-facsimile edition, New York: Horizon and Bramhall House, 1965.

Reprints Wright's three major essays entitled "In the Cause of Architecture" (1908, 1914, 1925), as well as an Introduction by the editor who sponsored the project, H. Th. Wijdeveld, and essays by Lewis Mumford, H. P. Berlage, J. J. P. Oud, Rob. Mallet-Stevens, Erich Mendelsohn, Louis Sullivan, and Wright himself. Considered by Wright to be the most beautiful publication of his work, it also provides extensive photographic coverage of the buildings between the late prairie houses and 1925.

1930   *Modern Architecture, Being the Kahn Lectures for 1930.* Princeton, 1931. Reprinted without the original illustrations in Frank Lloyd Wright, *The Future of Architecture* (New York: Horizon, 1953), pp. 67–182.

1931   *Two Lectures on Architecture.* Chicago: Art Institute. Reprinted in Frank Lloyd Wright, *The Future of Architecture* (New York: Horizon, 1953), pp. 183–219.

1932   *An Autobiography.* London: Longmans, Green. Revised and enlarged edition, New York: Duell, Sloan and Pearce, 1943; an index to this version has been published in Linn Ann Cowles, *An Index and Guide to "An Autobiography," the 1943 Edition, by Frank Lloyd Wright* (Hopkins, Minn., 1976). Third revised edition, New York: Horizon, 1977.

1938 Special issue of *Architectural Forum* 68 (January 1938): 1–102, devoted to the work of Wright.

The best source for photographs and for Wright's own ideas on his comeback of the thirties, with extensive coverage of Taliesin, Fallingwater, and the Johnson buildings in Racine, Wisconsin.

2. GENERAL BOOKS

Brooks, H. Allen, ed. *Writings on Wright.* Cambridge, Mass.: M.I.T. Press, 1981.

An unusual and sympathetic anthology of writings by friends, critics, architects, and scholars, with above all a moving and very prophetic essay by Louis Mumford written in 1929.

———. *The Prairie School: Frank Lloyd Wright and His Midwest Contemporaries.* Toronto: University of Toronto Press, 1972.

Brings Wright into clearer focus by studying the work of his followers.

Eaton, Leonard K. *Two Chicago Architects and Their Clients: Frank Lloyd Wright and Howard Van Doren Shaw.* Cambridge, Mass.: M.I.T. Press, 1969.

A brilliant study of Wright's patrons in their historical context.

Hanks, David. *The Decorative Designs of Frank Lloyd Wright.* New York: E. P. Dutton, 1979.
New facts on furniture and the decorative arts.

Hitchcock, Henry-Russell. *In the Nature of Materials: The Buildings of Frank Lloyd Wright, 1887–1941.* New York: Duell, Sloan, and Pearce, 1942. Reprint, New York: Da Capo, 1973.

The official biography and now a classic, with illustrations chosen by Wright himself. Contains a valuable list of works up to 1941, with addresses, that is still useful for the traveler. The perceptive text should be supplemented by the same author's article "Frank Lloyd Wright and the 'Academic Tradition' of the early Eighteen-Nineties," *Journal of the Warburg and Courtauld Institutes* 7 (1944): 46–63.

Jordy, William. *Progressive and Academic Ideals at the Turn of the Twentieth Century,* pp. 180–216. Vol. 3 of *American Buildings and Their Architects,* edited by W. Pierson. New York: Doubleday, 1972.

———. *The Impact of European Modernism in the Mid-Twentieth Century,* pp. 279–359. Vol. 4 of *American Buildings and Their Architects,* edited by W. Pierson. New York: Doubleday, 1972.

These two chapters occupy a unique place for their clarity, keen vision and breadth of context. They focus on the Robie House and the Guggenheim Museum, but range widely over all of Wright's work.

Manson, Grant. *Frank Lloyd Wright to 1910: The First Golden Age.* New York: Reinhold, 1958. Reprint, New York: Van Nostrand Reinhold, n.d.

Readable, well illustrated, nearly complete, and still the best guide to the buildings up to 1910.

Scully, Vincent. *Frank Lloyd Wright.* New York: Braziller, 1960.

Short but imaginative.

Smith, Norris Kelley. *Frank Lloyd Wright: A Study in Architectural Content.* Englewood Cliffs: Prentice-Hall, 1966. Reprint, Watkins Glen, N.Y.: American Life Foundation, 1979.

Highly interpretive, posing interesting questions but answering them in terms of the author's personal Christian world view.

Twombly, Robert C. *Frank Lloyd Wright: An Interpretive Biography.* New York: Harper and Row, 1973. 2d ed., New York: John Wiley and Sons, 1979.

Thin on the buildings, but full of new facts and often unusually perceptive on Wright the man.

3. MONOGRAPHS ON BUILDINGS

Hanna, Paul R., and Jean S. Hanna. *Frank Lloyd Wright's Hanna House.* Cambridge, Mass.: M.I.T. Press, 1981.

This and the book by Jacobs are accounts by clients that convey the adventure of building a

Wright house. They are detailed, well-documented primary sources but not analytic studies.

Hoffmann, Donald. *Frank Lloyd Wright's Fallingwater: The House and Its History.* New York: Dover, 1978.

> The best monograph.

Jacobs, Herbert, with Katherine Jacobs. *Building with Frank Lloyd Wright.* San Francisco: Chronicle Books, 1978.

4. EXHIBITION CATALOGS

Bulletin of the Metropolitan Museum of Art, Fall 1982.

> This issue of the Museum's bulletin is devoted to the collection of Frank Lloyd Wright material, including its recently installed showpiece, the living room of the Francis W. Little House of 1912. Text by R. Craig Miller, commentary by Edgar Kaufmann, Jr., and a very informative note on ''Frank Lloyd Wright and Japanese Prints'' by Julia Meech-Pekarik.

Several hundred drawings by Wright and his assistants are now available through two well illustrated exhibition catalogs.

Drexler, Arthur. *The Drawings of Frank Lloyd Wright.* New York: Horizon Press for the Museum of Modern Art, 1962.

> Contains a short but perceptive introduction.

Izzo, Alberto, Camillo Gubitosi, and Marcello Angrisani. *Frank Lloyd Wright Disegni.* Florence: Centro Di, 1976.

> Catalog of an exhibition of photographs of Wright's drawings held in the Palazzo Reale in Naples. The text has been translated into French and English in separate editions, but the main value of the book lies in the color reproductions.

5. GUIDEBOOKS

For the traveler about to embark on a Wright tour, there are now several useful guidebooks, in addition to the oeuvre list (with addresses) cited above in Henry-Rus-sell Hitchcock, *In the Nature of Materials: The Buildings of Frank Lloyd Wright, 1887–1941* (New York, 1942), pp. 107–30.

Sprague, Paul. *Frank Lloyd Wright and Prairie School Architecture in Oak Park.* 2d ed. Chicago: Follett, 1978.

Storrer, William Allin. *The Architecture of Frank Lloyd Wright: A Complete Catalogue.* Cambridge, Mass.: M.I.T. Press, 1974. 2d ed., 1978.

6. SELECTED ARTICLES

Brooks, H. Allen. ''Frank Lloyd Wright and the Wasmuth Drawings.'' *Art Bulletin* 48 (1966): 193–202.

Collins, George. ''Broadacre City: Wright's Utopia Reconsidered.'' In *Four Great Makers of Modern Architecture,* pp. 55–75. New York: Columbia University Press, 1963.

Hoffman, Donald. ''Frank Lloyd Wright and Viollet-le-Duc.'' *Journal of the Society of Architectural Historians* 28 (1969): 173–83.

Kaufmann, Edgar, Jr. ''Frank Lloyd Wright: Plasticity, Continuity, and Ornament.'' *Journal of the Society of Architectural Historians* 37 (1978): 34–39.

———. ''Precedent and Progress in the Work of Frank Lloyd Wright.'' *Journal of the Society of Architectural Historians* 39 (1980): 145–49.

> These are two recent contributions from among the many articles by Edgar Kaufmann, Jr., that combine the perspective of historian, Wright-trained architect, and owner of Fallingwater.

Levine, Neil. ''Frank Lloyd Wright's Diagonal Planning.'' In Helen Searing, ed., *In Search of Modern Architecture: A Tribute to Henry-Russell Hitchcock,* pp. 245–77. Cambridge, Mass.: M.I.T. Press, 1982.

O'Gorman, James F. ''Henry Hobson Richardson and Frank Lloyd Wright.'' *Art Quarterly* 32 (1969): 292–315.

Smith, Kathryn. ''Frank Lloyd Wright, Hollyhock House, and Olive Hill.'' *Journal of the Society of Architectural Historians* 38 (1979): 15–33.

Tselos, Dimitri. ''Exotic Influences in the Architecture of Frank Lloyd Wright.'' *Magazine of Art* 46 (April 1953): 160–69.

7. THE ROBIE HOUSE

The Robie House is mentioned in all books on Wright, but the best in-depth treatment is contained in the chapter in Jordy, *Progressive and Academic Ideals*, mentioned above (sec. 2). It should be read together with the same author's chapter on the Guggenheim Museum in *The Impact of European Modernism* (see above) as a model study of two key buildings.

The facts of the commission were recalled by Robie with the help of his son in an interview of 1958, "Mr. Robie Knew What He Wanted," *Architectural Forum* 109 (October 1958): 126–27, 206, and 210, reprinted in Leonard K. Eaton, *Two Chicago Architects and Their Clients: Frank Lloyd Wright and Howard Van Doren Shaw* (Cambridge, Mass.: M.I.T. Press, 1969), pp. 126–33. Recently this information has been supplemented by an interview with Robie's daughter in Irma Strauss, "An Interview with Lorraine Robie O'Connor," *Frank Lloyd Wright Newsletter* 3, no. 4 (1980): 1–3.

The original interview was part of a flurry of publicity surrounding the house following the announcement of demolition plans by its owner, the Chicago Theological Seminary, in 1957. In 1958 it was purchased for $125,000 by Webb and Knapp, the realty company headed by William Zeckendorf, to be saved and used as headquarters for the firm's Hyde Park project. According to Zeckendorf, his friend Wright planned to take it over with his foundation but died too soon. An alternative was to give it to the National Trust for Historic Preservation. Finally the house was deeded to the University of Chicago, first as the seat for the Adlai Stevenson Institute for International Peace, then as the headquarters of the University Development Office. See "A Famous House Rescued," *Architectural Forum* 108 (February 1958): 69; William Zeckendorf, with Edward McCreary, *The Autobiography of William Zeckendorf* (New York, 1970), p. 242; "Robie House Restoration Underway," *Progressive Architecture* 46 (October 1965): 55–56; and the exhibition catalogue of Robie and other furniture prepared by the Committee of Architectural Heritage of the University of Illinois, *Frank Lloyd Wright: Vision and Legacy* (Urbana, 1966).

In 1978 William Barnard, son of the original contractor, generously donated the following documentary material to the Department of Special Collections of the University of Chicago Library:

1. The original blueprints of the house, as revised March 23, 1909, and including later pencil changes by Wright in the area of the balcony.

2. A survey of Robie's lot by Emil Rudolph dated March 18, 1909, labeled as being from book 397, page 68, no. 6403, with the following information: "Lot 16 and the S. 10 feet of lot 17 in Gray and Gaylord's sub. of Block 71 and W. ½ of Block 62 in Hopkin's Add. to Hyde Park, a sub. of W. ½ of N.E. ¼ of Sec. 14, Tp. 38N, R. 14 E. of the 3rd Principal Meridian." (See the map of 1871 illustrated in Jean Block, *Hyde Park Houses: An Informal History, 1856–1910* (Chicago: University of Chicago Press, 1978, p. 18, fig. 7.)

3. A set of the original specifications.

4. An account book with payments recorded between April 15, 1909, and June 21, 1910, for materials, labor, millwork, and hardware. A modern total of the payments amounts to $26,516.19.

5. Copies of 30 photographs of the house in construction, some of which have been published in "Frederick C. Robie House, Frank Lloyd Wright, Architect," *Prairie School Review* 4, no. 4 (1967): 10–19.

Working drawings for the furniture and rugs ordered from the Niedecken-Walbridge firm of Milwaukee are now in the Prairie School Archives at the Milwaukee Art Center. They are discussed and partly illustrated in David Hanks, *The Decorative Designs of Frank Lloyd Wright* (New York: E. P. Dutton, 1979), pp. 105–10 and 215–17. In addition, a large working drawing of the trim in the area of the staircase behind the living room chimney is in the John Lloyd Wright collection in Avery Library, Columbia University.

Measured drawings of the house and some of its furnishings were prepared by the Historic American Buildings Survey in 1963 and published as *The Robie House: Frank Lloyd Wright* (Palos Park, Ill., 1968).